BACKYARD GAMES

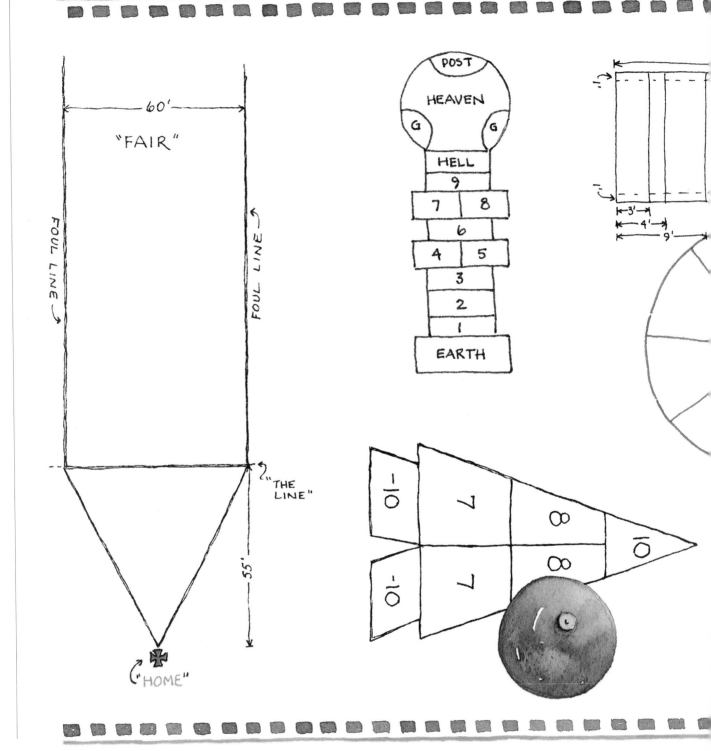

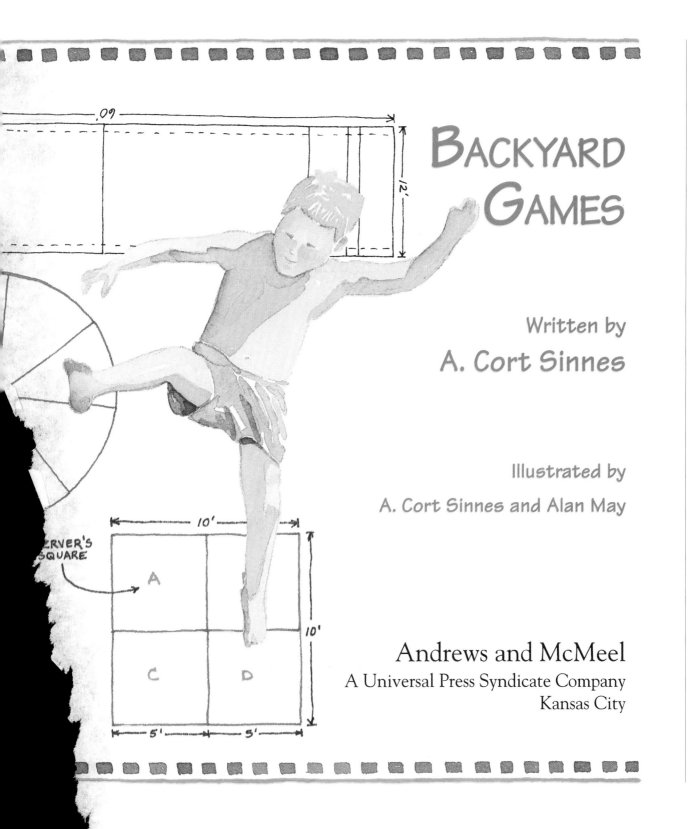

BACKYARD GAMES

Written by

A. Cort Sinnes

Illustrated by

A. Cort Sinnes and Alan May

Andrews and McMeel

A Universal Press Syndicate Company

Kansas City

5,

Attention: Schools and Businesses
Andrews and McMeel books are available at quantity discounts with
bulk purchase for educational, business, or sales promotional use. For
information, write to: Special Sales Department, Andrews and McMeel,
4900 Main Street, Kansas City, Missouri 64112.

This book was designed and produced by
Hearth & Garden Productions
A. Cort Sinnes, Designer
Christine Beyer, Production Manager

Project Editor, Harriet Choice
Copy Editor, Matt Lombardi

Library of Congress Cataloging-in-Publication Data

Sinnes, A. Cort
Backyard Games/written and illustrated by A. Cort Sinnes
    p.   cm.
Includes index.
ISBN 0-8362-4503-2 : $14.95
1. Games—Encyclopedias. 2. Games—Rules. I. Title
GV1201.S53 1992   92-46870
790.1'91--dc20   CIP

5/93 $ 890

For Blaine, Brooke, and Nels,
the best backyard kids around

Acknowledgments

To Katie, for helping me not lose my marbles, and to Brooke, for making me toe the line.

To Donna Martin, Harriet Choice, Dorothy O'Brien, Matt Lombardi, Claire LePlant, and Traci Bertz of Andrews and McMeel for their support, advice, and professionalism.

To Alan May, for knowing how to paint people and cheerfully agreeing to a collaborative effort—not to mention solving the "olly, olly oxen free" mystery.

To Christine Beyer, for her help from afar and her command of electronic wizardry.

To Lawrence Gazlay of General Sportcraft, for the knowledge at his fingertips and his willingness to help.

To the Runnions, in whose backyard much of this book actually took place.

To Arthur and Pinky Kase, for opening new doors onto more backyard fun.

To Warren Maus, for knowing the ins and outs of the hoops.

To Gina Gilbreth, for her happy snappies and her fun-loving sons.

To the following associations: United States Badminton Association, International Bocce Association, United States Croquet Association, American Lawn Bowls Association, National Horseshoe Pitchers Association, American Shuffleboard Association, and United States Volleyball Association, for their knowledgeable and good-natured assistance.

Thanks to all of you for helping me stay in the game and making sure I played by the rules.

"If any of the rules and regulations found in this book don't jibe with the way you play in your own backyard, you have my permission to play any ol' way you like."

CONTENTS

To this day, the question remains unanswered: What happens when the shuffleboard pucks go overboard?

PROLOGUE—SUMMER, 1964

e and my friends play games all the time. We play games on the sidewalk, in swimming pools, on our bicycles, riding in cars, in big trees, out in the field behind our house, and on the lawn in our backyard. I bet there isn't any place where we haven't played a game.

The lawn in our backyard is big enough to put up the whole croquet set. That's what we usually play after dinner. Even when we can't find all the pieces. Sometimes my parents play with us, but usually it's just me and my friend Jonathan. He lives across the street. We don't really know all the rules, but it's fun when you get to knock the other guy's ball as far off the lawn as you can. I think that's in the rule book.

I got a badminton set for my birthday. At first I didn't think it was going to be much fun, but it's pretty easy to play. You can really wail on that shuttlecock thing and make it fly. Jonathan almost always wins when we play croquet. I win the most at badminton.

I have another friend who lives in the country. He has a swimming pool. I ride my bike over there a lot. His dad had a shuffleboard court painted on the patio next to the pool. Tim, that's my friend's name, said the concrete had to be real smooth so the puck could slide from one end to the other. My dad says they play shuffleboard on ships. I wonder if the puck ever goes over the side of the ship? Sometimes when we play at Tim's house, the puck lands in the pool. But at least we can jump in and get it off the bottom.

I like playing games at home, but it's a different story at school. In P.E. I'm always about the last one to get picked, especially when we play softball and football. I have a friend who's always a captain, no matter what game we have to play. He picks me just before there's no one else left so I won't feel bad. He's a nice guy. He made up a new position for me when we have to play softball. It's behind the other left fielder. It's pretty neat out there because I can just stand there in the sun and think about other stuff.

Except for one day.

Someone hit a ball really hard and I started to hear people call my name. The next thing I heard was the sound of the ball whizzing right toward me. I didn't have time to think about what to do, so I just stuck my glove out and the ball fell right in it. The best thing was it didn't fall out again. Later on, it was like I was a hero or something.

Every once in a while even the games in P.E. are okay. But still not as fun as the stuff we play at home.

A.C.S.
Summer, 1964

How long do you think it would take for the proverbial "caveman" to pick up the game of baseball? Probably not long. Timeless pursuits, indeed.

TIMELESS PURSUITS

With very few exceptions, every game we play today has its roots in ancient history. It seems that for as long as there have been humans in the world, there have been games.

The one aspect of games that *has* changed over the past several thousand years is why we play them. When primitive people first started throwing rocks at a target, it was to sharpen their hunting skills, not to score points. When the ancients tossed the dried knucklebones of sheep (a precursor to the modern game of jacks), it was an attempt to foresee the future, not merely a way of passing the time and increasing one's hand-eye coordination. And a tug-of-war between two communities a thousand years ago was not just for laughs, but for a sign from above, indicating whose rice harvest was going to be the best.

Today, the person looking for an excuse to play an outdoor game might be quick to point out the benefits of exercise and the lessons learned in any cooperative team effort. But the very fact that anyone would need an excuse to play a game may itself be an indication of misplaced priorities.

Someone once said that the purest form of relaxation is play. If that observation is true, then perhaps game-playing is every bit as significant for us today as it ever has been in the past, albeit for different reasons. If the playing of a game of croquet, a family reunion tug-of-war, or an extended session of flash-light tag on a warm summer night allows you, your family, or your friends to slow down for a moment, enjoy the company of those around you, and perhaps get in a good laugh or two, then game-playing has an important place in contemporary life. Games, and the fun that goes with them, may provide the

"Who said anything about relaxing? I play to win!"

Who's First?

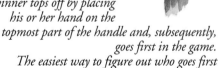

Over the years, a variety of methods have developed, more or less on their own, for determining who goes first in a game. One of the most time-honored is the toss of a coin. This method works best when there are only two people playing, or in situations where two team "captains" are chosen to determine who will play first. After calling what side they want (heads or tails), one of the participants (or a third party) flips a coin into the air, catches it in one hand, and flips it over onto the top of the other. Whichever side of the coin faces up determines who goes first. In case you were wondering, the designation "tails" refers to many of the coins from yesteryear, which commonly had a depiction of our national bird, the bald eagle, on the reverse of the "head" side; "tails," presumably, refers to its tail feathers.

Another time-honored method of choosing who goes first is to toss a baseball bat, handle end up, vertically into the air. The participants (it works best with two people, but three or more are possible) rush to grab the bat with one hand, each person placing their hand on top of the last hand laid on the bat, until there is no more room on the handle. The winner tops off by placing his or her hand on the topmost part of the handle and, subsequently, goes first in the game.

The easiest way to figure out who goes first amongst a group is to "draw straws." The "straws" can be straws plucked from a broom, drinking straws, small twigs, or wooden matches. Make sure you have one straw for each participant, with one that is clearly longer in length than the others. After tamping them so they appear to be all the same length, one person holds the straws in his or her hand, concealing the opposite ends. Each participant selects a straw; the one with the longest straw goes first.

light-hearted focus and laughter we so desperately need as balance in a world of weighty concerns.

Playing for Fun

One of the best aspects of backyard games—as opposed to games played at school and the world of professional sports—is that they can be played for no other reason than to have a good time.

All of us know certain people for whom simply having fun is a foreign concept. Put a racket in one of these people's hands, and a barefoot game of badminton quickly takes on the gravity of an Olympic trial match. While it's true that competition is an intrinsic part of any game (even if you are playing a game by yourself), when it comes to backyard games, the accent should definitely be on fun rather than competition. There are plenty of other places where strict competition has its rightful place; I say, leave it there, rather than on your backyard lawn.

If kids are a part of your backyard, they'll definitely be party to the games played there. Kids, especially, need to know that all the world is not an arena, and that there are times when it's okay just to hang out, have fun, and maybe even laugh at one's own mistakes. If you find yourself in the role of game facilitator or referee, a relaxed attitude on your part reinforces the notion of the backyard as a place to play, rather than a stadium where winning is all. With just a little bit of positive reinforcement in the fun department, there will be a lot more laughter than whining and tears.

And speaking of whining, adults have been known to do their fair share when asked (perhaps once too often) to procure a missing shuttlecock or to go to the local gas station to fill a ball with air. Thankfully, adult whining can be avoided by remembering the scout motto: "Be Prepared."

Handy to Have on Hand

It's no fun to have to run to the store to get that one missing something, especially when the trip necessitates a change of clothes, putting on shoes, and finding your wallet and keys just to get out the door. As the proprietor of your own backyard game and sports complex, you can make life a lot easier by keeping the following items on hand:

1) small air pump
2) metal inflation needle
3) chalk for marking lines
4) extra shuttlecocks
5) first aid kit
6) sunscreen
7) insect repellent
8) large, reusable plastic drink cups

If you have trouble keeping all the equipment needed for various games intact, keep your eyes open the next time you visit a garage sale. Someone else's incomplete badminton, croquet, bocce, or horseshoe set may be just what you need to round yours out back home. Undoubtedly, the price will be right, and you may even wind up with enough mallets, balls, and nets to invite the whole neighborhood over.

Storing Equipment

Playing a backyard game is often a spur-of-the-moment activity. And nothing dampens a whim faster than having to go search for equipment, or finding the supplies so ravaged that it's impossible to play the game. To avoid this, keep all of your backyard game supplies in one easily accessible spot, even if it's just a large cardboard box kept in the garage.

Every once in a while it's a good idea to round up all the boxes in which the equipment was originally packaged, try to find the instruction booklets, and check to see if you have a full set of croquet mallets, usable shuttlecocks, or a volleyball that still holds air. If there are missing pieces, carefully search the entire backyard. It's amazing how a badminton racquet will mysteriously appear from behind the shrubbery and how missing croquet balls show up, inexplicably, in the tree house. Scrupulously comb the lawn, because if there's one thing you never want to do, it's run over a horseshoe with a power lawn mower!

Making Marks

The best method for marking a hopscotch pattern on a sidewalk or concrete patio is to use chalk. Most variety stores carry specially

designated "sidewalk chalk," which comes in vibrant colors and is usually larger in size than the standard chalkboard variety. Although adults may gasp in horror when confronted with a marked-up patio, rest assured the chalk comes

off easily with a garden hose or the first rain.

When it comes to making marks on grass lawns, the old-fashioned method is to use ground limestone (sometimes sold in garden centers as "agricultural lime"). Although you don't see it much anymore, schools and some professional organizations still use ground limestone for indicating lines on lawns, but generally use a special wheeled applicator to lay down uniform, straight lines. In the absence of a limestone applicator, the white, powdery (harmless) substance can be "poured" from a large can in more or less uniform lines.

Better yet is the court-marking kit made by the General Sportcraft Company (140 Woodbine St. Bergenfield, New Jersey, 07621, 201/384-4242). It contains a skein of florescent-colored twine and four small plastic "flags." The flags are easily inserted into the turf, marking the corners of the court. The twine is then wrapped around the flags to indicate the perimeter of the playing field.

If all you need is something to mark the corners of a playing field, brightly colored pylons (illustrated on page 22) work great. As with the court-marking kit, the pylons are available from General Sportcraft.

An Ideal Backyard for Games

The backyard illustrated at right may be a fantasy, but if you really enjoy living and playing outdoors, you might want to incorporate some of its features into your own private "playground."

The large, level, rectangular lawn was laid out and planted with backyard games in mind. To start with, the outside dimensions of the lawn (30 feet by 60 feet) accommodate all backyard games—from badminton to volleyball. Although an "official" croquet court requires 50 by 100 feet, most aficionados agree that a 30-by-60-foot lawn allows enough room for an excellent game. If you have the opportunity to start your lawn from scratch, by all means keep the dimensions required for your favorite games in mind. And when it comes time to choose a grass variety, favor one of the "tougher" grasses that will hold up to heavy use.

Off to the left, in the shade, notice the "bleachers." It's always a good idea to provide seating (especially in the shade) for an audience. The more comfortable you make the seating, the longer the spectators will watch.

At the end of the walkway, you'll find another covered sitting area. Raised up a step or two, this centrally located structure is just the thing for an "awards ceremony." Alternately, it makes a great place to stage a play, or even a backyard wedding. When not in use for such auspicious events, it's just the spot to sit and enjoy the action on the field.

In the far left corner of this fantasy backyard there's a built-in barbecue. If you're planning a backyard for serious fun, better include a place to cook and a nice place to consume that hot-off-the-grill meal. There's nothing like an active day outdoors to work up a big appetite—and we all know someone who considers eating to be the best outdoor sport of all!

And as long as this is a fantasy, might as well include a swimming pool. There's nothing like one for cooling off after a demon game of volleyball, for playing any number of water sports, or that daily exercise routine.

Just like in a real backyard, there was only so much room in this fantasy one. Although they are not pictured in the illustration, here are a few other elements you might want to consider as you go about planning your own backyard:

• A shuffleboard, permanently marked on the patio or next to the pool

• An outdoor shower; great for before and after swimming

• A horseshoe pit or bocce court; good use of that long, narrow space in the side yard

• A spa, close by the pool, for soothing those "new" muscles you found playing a full set of badminton

A GALLERY OF BALLS

THE NUMBER OF VARIATIONS ON ONE THEME NAMELY THAT SPHERICAL OBJECT KNOWN AS A BALL IS TRULY AMAZING. THE ILLUSTRATIONS ON THESE TWO PAGES REPRESENT ONLY A SAMPLING, BUT IF YOU HAD ONLY ONE OF EACH, YOU D BE ABLE TO PLAY JUST ABOUT ANY BACKYARD GAME YOU COULD EVER DREAM UP. KEEP IN MIND THAT ANY BALL AIR-FILLED WILL LOSE SOME OF THAT AIR OVER TIME, AND THERE S NOTHING THAT CAN HALT A GAME OF VOLLEYBALL OR BASKETBALL FASTER THAN A FLAT BALL. SEE PAGE 22 FOR A COUPLE OF ITEMS TO KEEP ON HAND THAT WILL QUICKLY REMEDY THIS SITUATION.

BASEBALLS COME IN AN ASSORTMENT OF SIZES: THE SMALL HARDBALLS (BEST LEFT ON THE FIELD); THE LARGER (USUALLY 12 INCHES IN DIAMETER), SOFTER SOFTBALL; AND A VARIETY OF MODELS SPECIFICALLY DESIGNED FOR LITTLE LEAGUE PLAY. THE BIGGEST BASEBALL PICTURED HERE IS AN ANTIQUE, MADE FOR SOMETHING CALLED THE METROPOLITAN LEAGUE. INCREDIBLY, THIS OLD BALL HAS A DIAMETER OF MORE THAN 16 INCHES.

A RUBBER PLAY-GROUND BALL MAY BE ONE OF THE BEST ALL-PURPOSE BALLS YOU CAN KEEP ON HAND.

AN OFFICIAL VOLLEYBALL IS SPHERICAL, WITH A LACELESS LEATHER OR LEATHERLIKE, WATER-RESITANT COVER OF 18 PANELS COVERING A RUBBERLIKE BLADDER. THE PRESSURE OF THE BALL SHALL BE 5.0 LBS/SQ. IN. BALLS MAY BE WHITE, SOLID COLOR, OR MULTI-COLORED.

A TETHERBALL IS THE ONLY BALL THAT COMES WITH ITS OWN HANDLE.

PING-PONG BALLS BOUNCE LIKE NO OTHER BALL. IN A PINCH, THEY CAN BE USED FOR PLAYING JACKS.

IN ADDITION TO ITS ALL-IMPORTANT ROLE IN THE GAME OF SOCCER, A SOCCER BALL ALSO CAN STAND IN AS A KICKBALL OR A VOLLEYBALL.

CROQUET BALLS ARE MADE OF A VERY STURDY COMPOSITION MATERIAL OR SOLID WOOD, AND PAINTED WITH A STRONG, WATER-RESISTANT, CHIP-PROOF PAINT.

A BUNCH OF TENNIS BALLS, EVEN IF THEY RE A LITTLE FLAT, ARE GOOD TO KEEP ON HAND FOR USE IN IMPROVISING ANY NUMBER OF GAMES.

SIMILAR IN SIZE AND WEIGHT TO BOCCE BALLS, BALLS FOR PLAYING THE FRENCH GAME OF *JEU DE BOULES* ARE USUALLY MADE OF A COMPOSITION MATERIAL. A VARIATION OF BOULES PLAYED IN THE SOUTH OF FRANCE, CALLED *PETANQUE*, USES METAL BALLS. THE SMALLER TARGET BALL IS CALLED A *COCHONNET*.

IF YOU'RE WORRIED ABOUT BROKEN WINDOWS AND BLACKENED EYES, KEEP A READY SUPPY OF "WIFFLE" BALLS ON HAND.

LIKE OLD TENNIS BALLS, USED GOLF BALLS ARE GREAT TO HAVE ON HAND FOR IMPROVISING OTHER GAMES, OR EVEN FOR A ROUND OF MINIATURE GOLF.

INFLATABLE BEACH BALLS HAVE NO OFFICIAL ROLE IN ANY GAME, BUT THAT DOESN'T MEAN THAT THEY'RE NOT FUN TO KNOCK AROUND—AND THEY CERTAINLY WON'T HURT ANYTHING OR ANYONE. BEACH BALLS ALSO WORK AS A SUBSTITUTE FOR VOLLEYBALLS, ESPECIALLY FOR THE YOUNGER SET.

THE BALLS FOR PLAYING LAWN BOWLS ARE CALLED "BOWLS" AND ARE PROBABLY THE MOST UNUSUAL BALLS MADE, OWING TO THE FACT THAT THEY INTENTIONALLY ROLL IN AN ARC, RATHER THAN A STRAIGHT LINE. BOWLS COME IN A VARIETY OF SIZES AND WEIGHTS, AND SHOULD BE CHOSEN WITH COMFORT IN MIND.

WHILE THERE SEEMS TO BE CONSIDERABLE CONTROVERSY OVER WHAT CONSTITUTES AN OFFICIAL BOCCE BALL, IF YOUR BOCCE PLAYING IS CONFINED TO YOUR BACKYARD, IT DOESN'T REALLY MATTER WHAT SIZE BALL YOU USE. THE SMALLER TARGET BALL IS KNOWN AS A *PALLINO*.

NOTHING REALLY TAKES THE PLACE OF A BASKETBALL. ITS SIZE, WEIGHT, AND TEXTURED COVER MAKE IT A UNIQUE PIECE OF EQUIPMENT. IF YOU PLAY BASKETBALL REGULARLY, KEEP A HAND AIR PUMP, AN INFLATING NEEDLE, AND A PRESSURE GAUGE ON HAND (SEE PAGE 22); A BASKETBALL SEEMS TO HAVE A PECULIAR HABIT OF LOSING AIR JUST WHEN YOU NEED IT THE MOST.

BATS, RACKETS, MALLETS, AND OTHER EQUIPMENT

CROQUET EQUIPMENT IS AVAILABLE IN A WIDE VARIETY OF STYLES AND QUALITY, FROM INEXPENSIVE TO DEFINITELY PRICEY. THE GAME HAS BECOME QUITE POPULAR IN THIS COUNTRY, AND SEVERAL MAIL-ORDER COMPANIES NOW OFFER PROFESSIONAL QUALITY SETS IMPORTED FROM ENGLAND (SEE PAGE 123). ALTHOUGH EXPENSIVE, THEY ARE BEAUTIFULLY CRAFTED AND BUILT TO LAST A GENERATION OR TWO. ILLUSTRATED HERE ARE THREE TYPES OF CROQUET WICKETS. YOU DIDN'T KNOW THERE WERE DIFFERENT KINDS? SEE PAGE 37 FOR MORE INFORMATION.

ALTHOUGH IT'S POSSIBLE TO PLAY HORSESHOES WITH SHOES TAKEN RIGHT OFF A HORSE, SPECIAL PITCHING SHOES HAVE BEEN MADE FOR THIS GAME SINCE THE 1920s. USE OF THESE SO-CALLED "OPEN SHOES" HAS RESULTED IN A HIGHER PERCENTAGE OF RINGERS PER GAME. SEE PAGE 47 FOR MORE INFORMATION.

GOOD BADMINTON RACKETS ARE RELATIVELY LIGHT IN WEIGHT, BUT STURDY AND WELL-BALANCED. LIKE CROQUET EQUIPMENT, THEY ARE AVAILABLE IN A WIDE RANGE OF QUALITY AND PRICES.

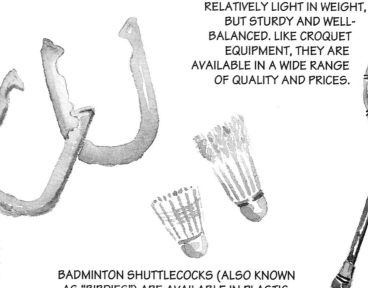

BADMINTON SHUTTLECOCKS (ALSO KNOWN AS "BIRDIES") ARE AVAILABLE IN PLASTIC, NYLON, AND THE TRADITIONAL FEATHERED MODELS. PLASTIC AND NYLON TYPES ARE RECOMMENDED FOR OUTDOOR PLAY.

TODAY'S BASEBALL BATS ARE MADE OF EVERYTHING FROM WOOD, TO METAL ALLOYS, TO PLASTIC. IT'S A GOOD IDEA TO HAVE A COUPLE OF BATS ON HAND, ESPECIALLY THE INEXPENSIVE, PLASTIC TYPES: THEY COME IN HANDY FOR A VARIETY OF ACTIVITIES (SUCH AS THE GOOFBALL GAMES ON PAGE 70) AND ARE EASY FOR YOUNGSTERS TO HANDLE.

IF YOU HAVE A SPOT FOR A BASKETBALL HOOP—SUCH AS OVER THE GARAGE DOOR—BY ALL MEANS PUT ONE UP. THEY'RE GREAT FOR IMPROMPTU HALF-COURT GAMES OR FOR PLAYING H-O-R-S-E (SEE PAGE 46).

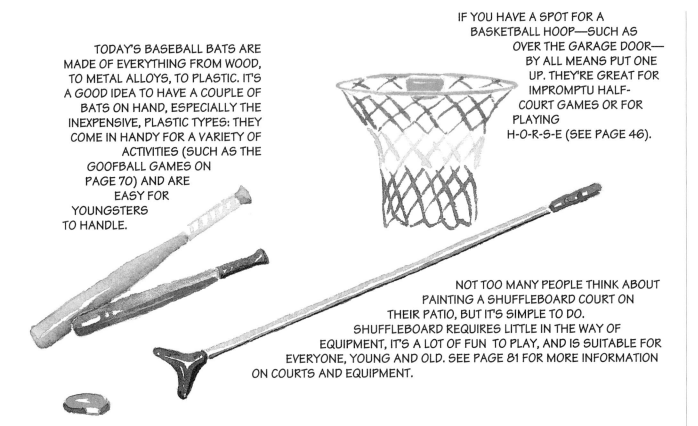

NOT TOO MANY PEOPLE THINK ABOUT PAINTING A SHUFFLEBOARD COURT ON THEIR PATIO, BUT IT'S SIMPLE TO DO. SHUFFLEBOARD REQUIRES LITTLE IN THE WAY OF EQUIPMENT, IT'S A LOT OF FUN TO PLAY, AND IS SUITABLE FOR EVERYONE, YOUNG AND OLD. SEE PAGE 81 FOR MORE INFORMATION ON COURTS AND EQUIPMENT.

ALTHOUGH MOST GAMES HAVE REGULATION OR OFFICIAL SIZE NETS, IF YOU'RE NOT A STICKLER FOR DETAILS, HAVING JUST ONE NET ON HAND WILL ALLOW YOU TO PLAY AERIAL TENNIS, BAD-MINTON, AND VOLLEYBALL, NOT TO MENTION ANY OTHER GAME YOU MIGHT THINK UP.

MISCELLANEOUS SUPPLIES

WITH THE EXCEPTION OF THE WHISTLE, THE ITEMS ILLUSTRATED ON THIS PAGE SHOULD PROBABLY BE CONSIDERED NECESSITIES RATHER THAN MISCELLANEOUS SUPPLIES. AFTER ALL, WHILE IT'S POSSIBLE TO YELL INSTEAD OF USING WHISTLE, IT'S MIGHTY HARD TO BLOW UP A VOLLEYBALL WITH JUST YOUR LIPS AND A LOT OF WIND. WITH THAT IN MIND, IT'S A GOOD IDEA TO KEEP EACH OF THESE SUPPLIES ON HAND, ALL IN ONE SECURE PLACE.

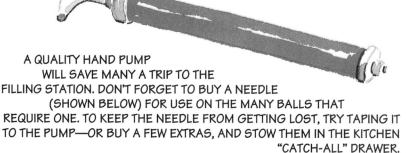

A QUALITY HAND PUMP WILL SAVE MANY A TRIP TO THE FILLING STATION. DON'T FORGET TO BUY A NEEDLE (SHOWN BELOW) FOR USE ON THE MANY BALLS THAT REQUIRE ONE. TO KEEP THE NEEDLE FROM GETTING LOST, TRY TAPING IT TO THE PUMP—OR BUY A FEW EXTRAS, AND STOW THEM IN THE KITCHEN "CATCH-ALL" DRAWER.

FLORESCENT ORANGE PLASTIC PYLONS ARE EXCELLENT FOR MARKING "GOAL POSTS" OR THE BOUNDARIES OF A PLAYING FIELD. PRACTICALLY INDESTRUCTIBLE, THEY SHOULD LAST FOR MANY SEASONS.

NOTHING—NOT EVEN A BLACK AND WHITE STRIPED SHIRT—GIVES THE PERSON DESIGNATED AS "REFEREE" MORE CLOUT THAN A WHISTLE. IF YOU'RE GOING TO BUY ONE, BUY A GOOD, LOUD ONE, AND ASK SOMEONE TO MAKE A LANYARD FOR IT, SO YOU CAN HANG IT AROUND YOUR NECK AND REALLY LOOK SERIOUS.

ANOTHER HANDY ITEM TO HAVE AROUND IS A POCKET PRESSURE GAUGE, ESPECIALLY FOR THOSE WHO LIKE TO GET THINGS "RIGHT ON THE MONEY."

ENCYCLOPEDIA
OF GAMES

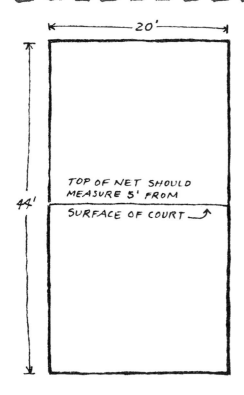

← 20' →

44'

TOP OF NET SHOULD
MEASURE 5' FROM

SURFACE OF COURT →

AERIAL TENNIS

AERIAL TENNIS IS A GREAT GAME FOR PEOPLE WHO ARE MORE CONCERNED WITH HAVING FUN THAN PLAYING BY THE RULES. THE MAIN REASON FOR THIS IS THAT THE GAME, SOMEWHAT SURPRISINGLY, COMES WITHOUT RULES. BE THAT AS IT MAY, MOST PEOPLE SIMPLY ADAPT THE RULES OF BADMINTON (SEE PAGE 27) ANY WAY THEY SEE FIT, AND SET ABOUT HAVING A GOOD TIME. BOTH THE WOODEN PADDLES AND THE SHUTTLECOCKS ARE STURDILY CONSTRUCTED; BEGINNING PLAYERS, BE THEY YOUNG OR OLD, WILL FIND THE EQUIPMENT EASY TO MASTER.

THE POPULARITY OF AERIAL TENNIS HAS BEEN DUE ENTIRELY TO WORD OF MOUTH, AS THE GAME IS NOT AVAILABLE AT RETAIL STORES, AND ONLY ONE COMPANY IN AMERICA MAKES THE EQUIPMENT. SEE TEXT AT RIGHT FOR MORE INFORMATION.

SHUTTLECOCKS FOR
AERIAL TENNIS HAVE
HEAVY RUBBER BASES
AND STURDY FEATHERS.

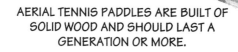

AERIAL TENNIS PADDLES ARE BUILT OF
SOLID WOOD AND SHOULD LAST A
GENERATION OR MORE.

ACS
1992

Aerial Tennis

Aerial tennis is a little-known game that deserves much greater popularity. A cross between badminton, volleyball, and Ping-Pong, it's perfect for backyard play. Aside from being fun, aerial tennis is very easy to learn to play—and play well. Even those totally unfamiliar with the game can become proficient in a single afternoon.

A generation ago, aerial tennis achieved regional popularity as an indoor game at community centers and athletic clubs. Enthusiasts soon found that aerial tennis could be just as successfully played outdoors, using a variety of court sizes and rules.

Aerial tennis is played with a sturdy, well-balanced wooden paddle, something like an elongated Ping-Pong paddle (about 18 inches long). Instead of a ball, the game is played with a heavy-duty shuttlecock (or "birdie").

For outdoor play, most people simply use the rules for badminton (see page 27), although the rules for Ping-Pong or even tennis could also be substituted (somewhat surprisingly, the game does not come with rules). As with tennis, aerial tennis may be played with singles (one person per side), or doubles (two teams of two).

Limiting the popularity of the game may be the fact that it is only available from one source (Sells Aerial Tennis Co., P.O. Box 4663, Springfield, Missouri, 65804), a source that doesn't advertise or promote the sport. Why not be the first on your block to play this little-known game?

"The tennis part I understand. But what do you do with the aerial?"

BADMINTON

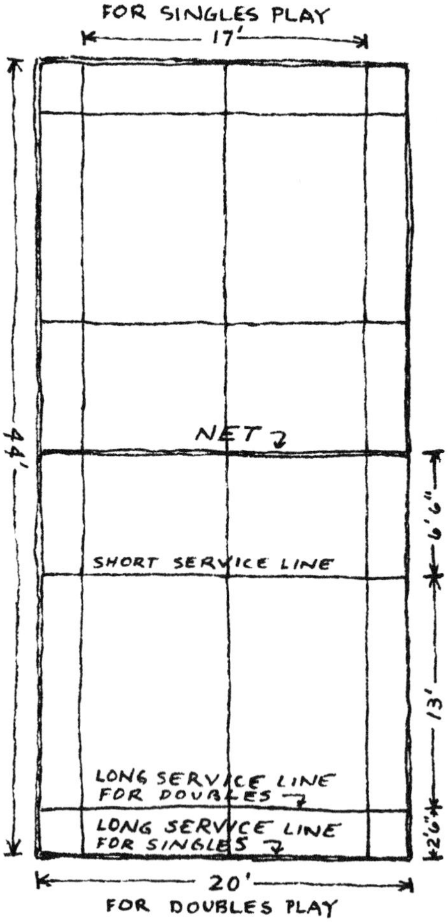

Court Diagram

FOR SINGLES PLAY
17'

44'

NET

SHORT SERVICE LINE

6'6"

13'

LONG SERVICE LINE FOR DOUBLES

LONG SERVICE LINE FOR SINGLES

2'6"

20'
FOR DOUBLES PLAY

Body Text

BADMINTON IS GENERALLY VIEWED AS A GENTEEL, NON-STRENUOUS GAME: NOT SO! BOTH SINGLES AND DOUBLES GAMES OFFER ENOUGH ACTION AND EXERCISE FOR EVEN THE MOST ATHLETICALLY ACCOMPLISHED. BADMINTON IS ALSO ONE OF THE FEW FORMAL OUTDOOR GAMES YOUNGSTERS FIND EASY TO MASTER, MAKING IT A GOOD CROSS-GENERATIONAL SPORT.

ALTHOUGH OFFICIAL TOURNAMENTS ARE PLAYED ON INDOOR COURTS, FEW PEOPLE WOULD DISAGREE THAT BADMINTON IS ONE OF THE ALL-TIME GREAT OUTDOOR GAMES. AN OFFICIAL BADMINTON COURT (17 FEET BY 44 FEET FOR SINGLES; 20 FEET BY 44 FEET FOR DOUBLES) EASILY FITS ON MOST BACKYARD LAWNS. SEE PAGE 15 FOR OPTIONS IN MARKING THE PERIMETER OF THE COURT.

COMPLETE BADMINTON SETS, WHICH INCLUDE RACKETS, NET, AND SHUTTLECOCKS, ARE WIDELY AVAILABLE AT SPORTING GOODS STORES. LARGER STORES WILL OFFER DIFFERENT QUALITY BADMINTON SETS IN A FAIRLY WIDE PRICE RANGE. INDOOR BADMINTON TOURNAMENTS ARE TRADITIONALLY PLAYED WITH FEATHERED SHUTTLECOCKS; OUTDOOR GAMES ARE BEST PLAYED WITH THEIR NYLON OR PLASTIC COUNTERPARTS.

AN OFFICIAL BADMINTON NET MEASURES 20 FEET LONG BY 30 INCHES WIDE. THE TOP OF THE NET, MEASURED IN THE MIDDLE OF THE COURT, SHOULD BE EXACTLY 61 INCHES FROM THE GROUND. AS WITH ANY GAME PLAYED ON A LAWN, IT'S BEST IF THE AREA IS LEVEL AND COMPLETELY FREE OF OBSTRUCTIONS. SPRINKLER HEADS, HOSE BIBS, AND THE LIKE SHOULD BE CLEARLY MARKED TO AVOID ACCIDENTS.

BADMINTON RACKETS ARE AVAILABLE IN MANY LEVELS OF QUALITY, FROM BEGINNER TO "PROFESSIONAL."

FEATHERED SHUTTLECOCK, TRADITIONALLY USED ONLY FOR INDOOR PLAY.

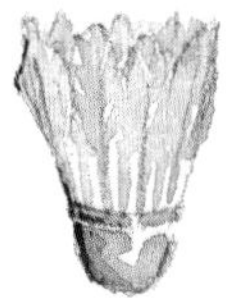

PLASTIC AND NYLON SHUTTLECOCKS ARE MADE TO STAND UP TO THE RIGORS OF OUTDOOR BADMINTON.

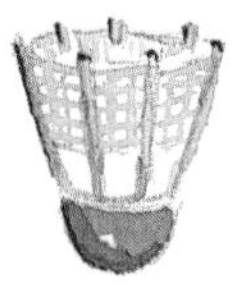

Badminton

Badminton has one of the richest and most varied histories of any game played today. Historians know that a game very much like badminton was played in ancient Greece and Egypt. More importantly, the act of hitting a shuttlecock with some kind of racket has been almost universal since time immemorial—except that instead of it being a sport, the activity was used to foretell the future. The number of times one could hit the shuttlecock straight into the air without missing would indicate the number of spouses one would have, the number of years one might live, and so forth.

Somewhere along the way, the soothsaying aspect of the shuttlecock and racket gave way to an organized game. And, like most good games, badminton eventually migrated to various corners of the world. In the 19th century, British army officers stationed in India took note of a game called *poona* (a game played with rackets and a shuttlecock), and took the game with them when they returned home. In 1873, *poona* was played on the grounds of the home of the Duke of Beaufort at Badminton, England. From that point on, the game was known as badminton.

Today, badminton is played in more than 70 countries worldwide. The International Badminton Federation oversees competitive matches. World Cup games are held every three years and, interestingly, are restricted to amateur players. Practice enough in your backyard and you could find yourself participating in a world-class competition!

With the exception of aerial tennis, badminton is the only game played with a shuttlecock, a half of a round piece of cork (or some other substance, such as plastic or nylon) with

*"Sometimes I hit the birdie so hard,
its feathers fall out."*

feathers stuck in the flat end. Hit with the small, light racket, the shuttlecock can travel straight through the air at speeds of more than 100 miles per hour, then suddenly slow down and drop to the ground. Although the game is easy for beginners to pick up, the curious behavior of the shuttlecock makes badminton a challenging game for the most fit and agile of athletes.

Official badminton games are played indoors, usually on a wooden floor. Most would agree that it is a much more pleasant game when played outdoors on a grass court. The official size for a badminton court is 17 by 44 feet, a size easily accommodated by most backyard lawns. For a doubles game (two players per side), the width of the court is expanded to 20 feet. The badminton net divides the center of the court. An official net is 20 feet long by 30 inches wide. The top of the net should measure exactly 61 inches from the ground.

In badminton, only the server can score a point. Play begins when the server, standing behind the baseline, serves the shuttlecock underhand. The serve must clear the net and fall within the boundaries of the court; failing to do so results in the serve alternating to the opposing player or team. After a successful serve, a point is scored if the receiving side fails to return the shuttlecock over the net or returns it out of bounds. If the server fails to return the shuttlecock over the net, or hits it out of bounds, the serve is granted to the opposite side. Play continues until one side scores either 15 or 21 points (decided upon before play begins).

The complete, official rules of badminton can be found on page 102.

Pictured above is the ancestral home of the Duke of Beaufort in Badminton, England. It was here, in 1873, that weekend guests of the Duke of Beaufort—certain British army officers, recently returned from India—played an Indian game known as poona. The game was played indoors, presumably on a rainy, typically English afternoon, with a rope stretched across a drawing room to serve as a net. Poona met with immediate popularity, and the game's name was changed to badminton, in honor of the place where it was first played in England.

Badminton, in addition to being the name of an estate, and in turn, the name of a game, is also the name of a drink. Although it has been a long time since anyone saddled up to the bar and ordered a "badminton," it was a very popular refreshment some 100 years ago. No less than the statesman Benjamin Disraeli pronounced badminton both "soothing and stimulating." The exact recipe for this concoction has been lost in the mists of time, but we know that it was made from claret, soda, spices and sugar—and light on the ice, one would imagine. Since the recipe is long gone, feel free to invent your own version of badminton—the drink. Who knows? You may start a new tradition.

Bocce

Bocce (or boccie, as it is sometimes spelled) is directly related to a similar game played in ancient Greece and Rome. The rules for bocce are so simple that any age group can play, but enough strategy and finesse are involved to keep it interesting day after day. Indeed, in many parts of Europe, you'll find the same group of people playing on public courts every day of the week, often in fierce competition.

Bocce is almost universally played on packed dirt or clay courts, some of which are filled with naturally occurring hazards like tree roots or immovable stones. Given this somewhat cavalier approach to the condition of the court, feel free to play bocce on the lawn, if you wish. The lawn will produce a different kind of action, but there's no rule that says you can't play bocce on a lawn.

Traditional courts are 12 by 60 feet long, although the measurements can be modified if the proportions are kept the same (such as 6 by 30 feet, or 8 by 45 feet).

The perimeter of a bocce court is usually defined with a short embankment (at least the height of a bocce ball, about 4⅜ inches), sturdy enough to withstand being hit by a speeding ball. Long lengths of two-by-six-inch lumber, well anchored to the ground, will do nicely. Proficient bocce players use the side and back walls for banking and rebound shots.

Bocce is played with eight large balls and one smaller target (or object) ball called the *pallino*. The game may be played one against one (four balls per person), with two two-person teams (two balls per person), two three-person teams (one ball per person), or with two four-person teams (one ball per person). The balls are made in two colors to distinguish the balls of one team from those of the other.

The object of the game is throw your balls closer to the pallino than your opponents do.

Traditionally, the toss of a coin determines which team throws the pallino. (For other methods, see "Who's First?" on page 14.) The pallino is thrown by a member of the team that won the coin toss. After throwing the pallino (which must be thrown at least half the distance of the court), the same player throws the first ball. The opposing team then delivers its bocce balls until one is nearer the pallino than the first team's ball, or until it has thrown all four of its balls. This "nearest ball" rule governs the sequence of thrown balls. The team whose ball is

Bocce Ball Controversy

For the past several years there has been considerable controversy over what constituted an "official" bocce ball. Thankfully, there has been an amicable resolution of sorts: the powers that be have decreed that individual leagues are free to determine what constitutes an official ball for their league. That said, most bocce purists claim a 113 mm (4½ inches diameter) is the real McCoy, while others insist that nothing but a 107 mm (4¼ inches diameter) ball will do. To confuse the matter further, those aren't the only two sizes of bocce balls available in this country. Your choices are illustrated here.

Scored, 113 mm composition balls

107 mm composition balls

Lacquer-finished 90 mm balls

4-inch plastic balls

107 mm metal balls

BOCCE

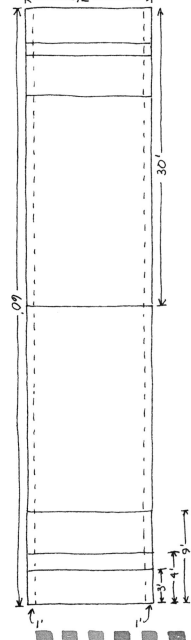

THE RECOMMENDED COURT SIZE FOR BOCCE IS 12 FEET WIDE BY 60 FEET LONG. VARIATIONS ARE ACCEPTABLE, PROVIDED FOUL LINES AND IN-BOUND MARKERS ARE CLEARLY ESTABLISHED.

THE COURT SURFACE MAY BE COMPOSED OF STONE DUST, PACKED DIRT, CLAY, GRASS, OR ARTIFICIAL TURF, PROVIDING THERE ARE NO PERMANENT OR TEMPORARY OBSTRUCTIONS IN THE COURT THAT WOULD INTERFERE WITH THE STRAIGHT LINE DELIVERY OF A BALL FROM ANY DIRECTION (IN PRACTICE, THIS IS NOT ALWAYS THE CASE).

THE SIDE AND END WALLS OF THE COURT MAY BE COMPOSED OF ANY MATERIAL THAT DOES NOT MOVE DURING PLAY AND IS AT LEAST AS HIGH AS A BOCCE BALL. THE SIDE OR END WALLS MAY BE UTILIZED FOR BANK SHOTS OR REBOUND SHOTS.

ALL COURTS SHOULD BE CLEARLY MARKED FOR THE FOLLOWING:

A) ONE FOOT FROM THE SIDE BOARDS—IN-BOUNDS FOR FIRST THROW OF THE PALLINO.

B) THREE FEET IN FROM EACH BACK BOARD—IN-BOUNDS FOR FIRST THROW OF PALLINO.

C) FOUR FEET FROM FEET FROM BACK BOARDS—FOUL LINE FOR POINTING. DISTANCE MAY VARY, IF FOUL LINES ARE CLEARLY MARKED.

D) NINE FEET FROM BACK BOARDS—FOUL LINE FOR SPOCKING OR HITTING. DISTANCE MAY VARY, IF FOUL LINES ARE CLEARLY MARKED.

E) HALF COURT LINE—MINIMUM DISTANCE PALLINO MAY BE THROWN ON FIRST THROW OF PALLINO. COURTS MAY HAVE ADDITIONAL MINIMUM DISTANCE LINES FOR THE PALLINO WHICH WOULD OVERRULE THE HALF COURT LINE. DURING THE COURSE OF PLAY, THE POSITION OF THE PALLINO MAY CHANGE AS A RESULT OF NORMAL PLAY; HOWEVER, THE PALLINO MAY NEVER COME TO REST CLOSER THAN THE HALF COURT LINE OR THE FRAME IS CONSIDERED DEAD.

A BOCCE BALL SET CONSISTS OF EIGHT BALLS AND A SMALLER, PALLINO (TARGET) BALL. ALTHOUGH THERE IS MUCH DISAGREEMENT REGARDING THE PROPER SIZE FOR A BOCCE BALL, MOST AGREE THAT A

PALLINO MUST NOT BE LARGER THAN 2½ INCHES IN DIAMETER (63 MM), NOR SMALLER THAN 1⅞ INCHES IN DIAMETER (48 MM). BY SOME MIRACLE, EVERYONE AGREES THAT THE PALLINO MUST BE A DISTINCTLY DIFFERENT COLOR THAN ANY OF THE BOCCE BALLS.

the closest to the pallino is called the "in" ball, and the opposing side the "out" ball. Whenever a team gets "in," it steps aside and allows the "out" team to bowl.

A team has the option of rolling, throwing, bouncing, or banking its ball down the court, provided it does not go out-of-bounds or the player does not violate the foul markers. A player also has the option of "spocking" or hitting out any ball in play in trying to obtain a point or to decrease the opposing team's points.

At the end of each frame (when both sides have played their four balls), a designated official, under the scrutiny of the "captain" of each team, determines the points scored. The balls scoring points are those closer to the pallino than the closest ball of the opposing team. This can be determined either by viewing or by mechanical measurement. Aficionados always use rulers!

In the event that the two balls closest to the pallino belong to opposing teams and are tied, no points will be awarded, and the pallino returns to the team that delivered it. Only balls distinguishably closer to the pallino than any opponent's balls may be awarded points.

The complete rules for bocce are mercifully short and simple. Before attempting to play bocce for the first time, consult the rules (which include the traditional system for scoring) on page 104.

Boules

The French game of jeu de boules (very similar to bocce) is sometimes shortened to just "boules." To be correct, however, the game should be called by its full name; please see page 51.

"What's the difference between bocce and jeu de boules?"

"Not much, except for the language."

31

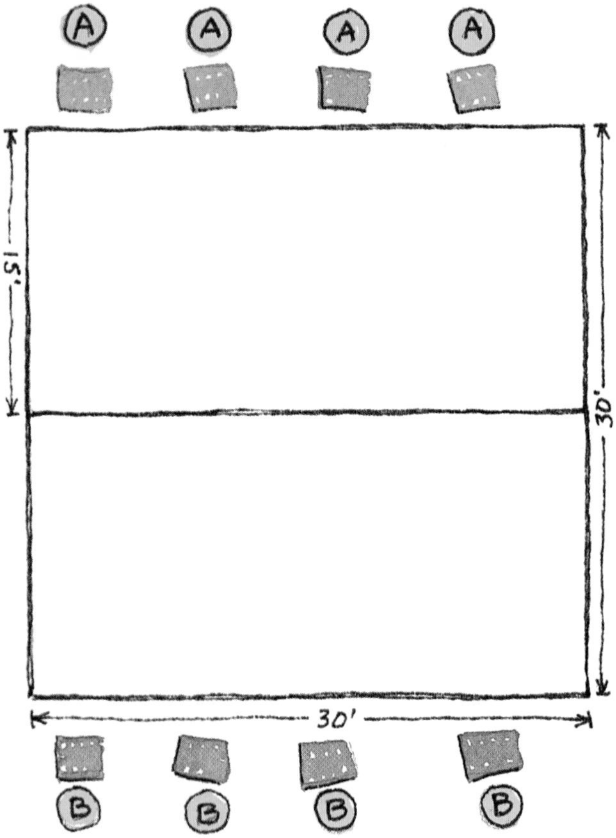

CAPTURE THE FLAG

ALTHOUGH THERE ARE MANY VARIATIONS OF THIS GAME—INCLUDING SOME WHERE THERE IS ONLY ONE "FLAG"—THE ONE SHOWN HERE IS THE BEST FOR BACKYARD PLAY. THE COURT SHOULD BE AT LEAST 30-FEET SQUARE; LARGER, IF YOU HAVE THE ROOM. MAKE SURE TO MARK THE CENTER LINE WITH A ROPE, HOSE, OR WHAT HAVE YOU.

HANDKERCHIEFS, OF TWO DIFFERENT COLORS, MAKE GREAT FLAGS; LACKING THESE, RAGS, DISH TOWELS, OR EVEN TORN-UP SHEETS WILL SUFFICE. JUST MAKE SURE THE TWO TEAMS KNOW WHICH FLAGS BELONG TO WHICH TEAM.

WHILE YOU'RE AT IT, KEEP THAT GARDEN HOSE HANDY: PARTICIPANTS IN THIS GAME MAY NEED TO BE PERIODICALLY HOSED DOWN WHEN THE ACTION BECOMES TOO ROUGH AND TUMBLE!

15'

30'

30'

TWO ESSENTIALS FOR THIS GAME: A LOUD WHISTLE FOR THE REFEREE AND A FRESH CAN OF BANDAGES FOR THE MEDIC.

Capture the Flag

Capture the flag is a rock 'em—sock 'em action game, hard to referee, almost certain to result in a few scrapes or bruises, and pure, wanton recreation. Because it is so hard to referee, capture-the-flag is probably best reserved for players at least 10 and older. With players younger than that, most of the game could be spent trying to find out just who did what to whom, why, and what should be done about it. In other words, some amount of self-policing and adherence to the rules is mandatory for a successful game.

To play capture the flag, you'll need a large grassy area at least 30 by 30 feet square (don't try playing capture-the-flag on any hard surface), at least eight players, and a handkerchief (or acceptable cloth substitute) for each player, preferably in two different colors, one color for each team.

Mark the edges and the center line of the playing field (see page 15). Divide the participants into two equal teams. Individual teams line up along opposite ends of the playing field facing the center line, just behind their own end lines. Before starting the game, each teammate places his or her handkerchief just inside the end line. At the sound of a predetermined signal, both sides rush forward to try and capture the opposing team's handkerchiefs. (Note: Veteran capture-the-flag players will instruct a few of their teammates to hold back toward their own endline to keep opposing team members away from the flags.)

The object of the game is for one team to capture all the handkerchiefs (or "flags") of the opposing team. But hold on, it's not that simple …

If a player is tagged by an opposing team member while attempting to capture a handkerchief, the tagged player must

"If you're a bruise collector, like I am, you'll love this game!"

retreat to an area behind the opposing team's end line. Such "prisoners" are set free when one of their own teammates tags them. The act of freeing a teammate from behind enemy lines must not be combined, either immediately before or after, with the capture of a handkerchief. After freeing a teammate, both the former prisoner and his or her liberator must return to their side of the field before resuming handkerchief attacks.

While a teammate may be recovered from behind enemy lines, a captured handkerchief may not; once captured, it is the property of the opposing team (remember that old line—"to the victor, go the spoils"?). Captured handkerchiefs are deposited on the capturer's side of the field.

Once a player has captured an opposing team's handkerchief, that player is immune from being tagged while he or she runs the flag back across the center line.

While on their own side of the center line, a player cannot be tagged and sent to prison by the opposition.

Capture-the-flag games have been known to go on for so long that exhaustion, rather than capturing

As symbols, flags carry a lot of weight. That may be one of the reasons why players of "capture the flag" become so caught up in the game and play with such intensity. All flags, from the very beginning, have proclaimed something about their owner. As such, there is loyalty to a flag, even if it's just a red handkerchief proclaiming "my side."

all the flags, calls an end to the game. As an alternative, some folks prefer to play games of a predetermined length of time—say 10 or 12 minutes—the winner being whichever team has the greater number of the opposing team's flags in its possession when the whistle blows.

Croquet

Croquet is a game that inspires great passion in some people. Fierce croquet matches held between families have been known to go on for generations, from one year to the next. It is a timeless game, one that can be as simple or as complex as the players care to make it.

Unlike most other games, croquet's exact origins are not known. What *is* known is that a game very similar to croquet, called *paille-maille,* was played during the 1300s in France. It made its way to Ireland, and from there to England, where, interestingly, a London field where it was played is still known by the English version of *paille-maille*—namely, Pall Mall.

It wasn't until 1850 that the game became widely popular, when a London toymaker, John Jaques, manufactured a complete croquet set. Soon thereafter, Americans were introduced to croquet, and although over the last 100 years or so its popularity has waxed and waned, it has never completely fallen out of favor. What was once a highly refined game intended for the elite has now become a common, pleasant backyard pastime and one of the fastest-growing games in America.

Tournament croquet is played on a rectangular grass court, mowed to a height of only a quarter- to a half-inch. Keeping professional croquet courts in perfect condition requires the same meticulous attention as putting greens. Obviously, home croquet courts can be more relaxed and the court any size you want. If possible, the long sides of the rectangular court should be twice as long as the short sides. And if a court 50 by 100 feet is not possible, 30 by 60 feet will do. It's a size most aficionados agree is as small as the court can be and still allow challenging play. If you don't have that much room, or if your lawn is of an irregular shape, decrease the number of wickets or set them up in any pattern you like.

The object of croquet is to hit your ball through the course of wickets in the prescribed order. The first person to hit the

"What I really like best is to smash my brother's ball so hard that it goes all the way into the neighbor's yard."

35

finishing stake wins the game.

Croquet can be played in one of the following four ways:

Individual: Each person is on his or her own, with one ball; up to six people may play individual croquet.

Singles: Two people play against each other, each with a single ball.

Doubles: Two teams of two people, with each member of each team playing his or her own ball.

Triples: Two teams of three people, with each member of each team playing his or her own ball.

Toss a coin to determine the start of the game (or use one of the other methods described on page 14); the winner may decide to play first or second. In team competition, the individual order of play is determined by the colored stripes on the finishing stake; each colored stripe corresponds to the color of a ball already picked by the various team members. Start at the top to determine who will be the first to play.

The complete, official rules for croquet can be found on page 105. For such a seemingly simple game, be forewarned that the rules are quite complex. Somewhere along the way, players must decide for themselves whether they are going to play croquet "by the book," or by some other, simplified set of "house rules." To avoid disagreement, make sure everyone agrees to the approach before the game begins.

One practical approach to the rules is to start playing the simplest game possible. As questions or problems arise, look them up in the official rules. Over a period of time, you will progressively begin playing a more "official" version of the game, without having to digest the entire set of rules before you play your first game.

CROQUET

IN PRACTICE, THERE IS CONSIDERABLE VARIATION IN THE WAY A CROQUET COURSE IS LAID OUT. THE DETERMINING FACTOR, OF COURSE, IS THE SPACE AVAILABLE IN YOUR BACKYARD. THAT SAID, THE WAY THE STAKES AND WICKETS ARE ARRANGED IN THE ILLUSTRATION BELOW REPRESENTS THE TRADITIONAL AND ACCEPTED ARRANGEMENT. NO MATTER HOW YOU LAY OUT YOUR COURT, YOU SHOULD FOLLOW THE RECOMMENDED COURSE (INDICATED BY THE ARROWS), FROM ONE STAKE TO THE OTHER, AND BACK TO THE STARTING STAKE.

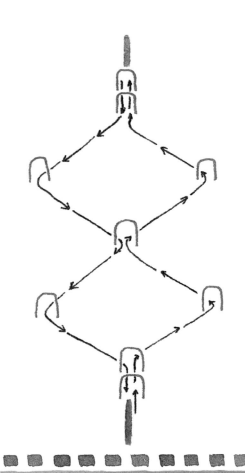

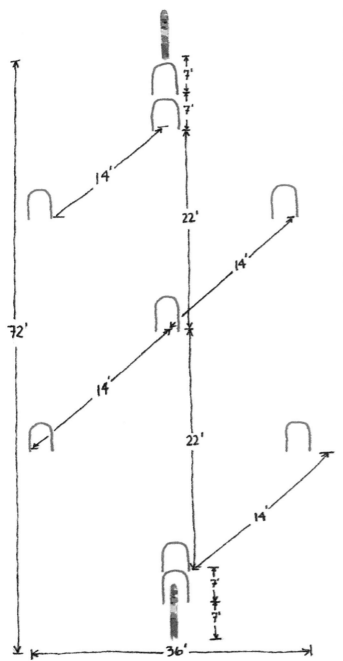

SHOWN AT LEFT IS THE RECOMMENDED SPACING FOR A 36-BY-72-FOOT CROQUET COURT. ALTHOUGH TOURNAMENT CROQUET GAMES TAKE PLACE ON 50-BY-100-FOOT COURTS, MOST BACKYARDS SIMPLY DO NOT HAVE LAWNS THAT LARGE. NO MATTER THE SIZE OF YOUR LAWN, ALWAYS MAKE THE CROQUET COURT AS LARGE AS POSSIBLE, AS IT MAKES FOR A MORE INTERESTING GAME. MAKE SURE THE LENGTH OF THE COURT IS TWICE THAT OF ITS WIDTH. EXPERTS GENERALLY AGREE THAT A 30-BY-60-FOOT CROQUET COURT IS THE MINIMUM SIZE FOR A GOOD GAME. LACKING A 100-FOOT TAPE MEASURE, LAY THE COURSE OUT BY FOOT (YOUR FOOT, THAT IS).

IF YOU EVER GET THE CHANCE, TAKE A LOOK AT AN OFFICIAL CROQUET COURT—IT IS A THING OF BEAUTY, NOT TO MENTION A MAINTENANCE NIGHTMARE! BASICALLY A HUGE PUTTING GREEN, OFFICIAL COURTS ARE ALMOST ALWAYS PLANTED WITH BENTGRASS, A VARIETY OF GRASS THAT CAN WITHSTAND VERY SHORT CLIPPING, USUALLY TO A HEIGHT OF ¼-INCH TO ½-INCH. DRAINAGE MUST BE PERFECT, WHICH USUALLY REQUIRES AN EXTENSIVE UNDERGROUND SYSTEM AND HUGE AMOUNTS OF SAND AS A BASE FOR THE GRASS. THINK TWICE BEFORE YOU DECIDE TO INSTALL A PROFESSIONAL COURT IN YOUR OWN BACKYARD!

THREE VARIETIES OF WICKETS: ON THE LEFT, THE U-SHAPED WIRE WICKET, WHICH COMES WITH MOST SETS AND HAS A 4- TO 6-INCH OPENING. SHOWN IN THE MIDDLE IS A "TOURNAMENT" OR "CHAMPIONSHIP" WICKET, USUALLY MADE OF CAST IRON, WITH AN OPENING ONLY 3¾-INCH WIDE. (NO WONDER THEY CALL IT A CHAMPIONSHIP WICKET!) ON THE RIGHT IS THE SO-CALLED "WINTER" WICKET (ALSO CALLED A CHALLENGE HOOP). MADE OF WROUGHT IRON, THE WINTER WICKET HAS ABOUT A 4-INCH OPENING.

Dodge Ball

There are many variations on dodge ball, the two most popular being standard dodge ball and circle dodge ball. To play, you'll need at least 10 players (for both variations), and a rubber playground ball, volleyball, or inflatable beach ball.

When the rules are explained to the players, be sure to add that it is customary for the person throwing the ball to aim low to avoid hurting anyone. This is one game where "hitting below the belt" is not only permissible, but encouraged.

The object of a standard dodge ball game is to eliminate the other team by hitting each opponent with the ball.

Begin by marking off a square playing court, about 30 feet square (see page 15). Mark all four sides and a center dividing line. Divide the group into two equal teams, and have them spread out on opposite sides of the center dividing line. Decide which team gets to throw first (see page 14).

The first team member throws the ball across the center line in an attempt to hit an opposing team member. If the ball hits the opponent, without the opponent catching the ball, he or she is "out," and leaves the court. The person who threw the "hit" gets to throw again. If the opposing team member catches the ball, the person who threw the ball is out, and leaves the court. The person who caught the ball throws the ball next.

If a ball is thrown to the opposite side without hitting anyone or being caught, the thrower gets to throw again.

All players must stay within the boundaries of the court at all times (except when retrieving the ball), and may not step over the center line. Anyone caught out of bounds is out of the game.

"Listen to me: When they say dodge, you dodge!"

In circle dodge ball, the object of the game is to be the last one left in the middle of the circle. To accomplish this, a player dodges the ball to avoid being hit.

Begin by dividing the players into two groups. Mark off a good-sized circle, and arrange one group outside the circle and the other group within it. The game starts when a player from the outside circle hurls the ball at someone inside the circle.

Players inside the circle are like those proverbial "sitting ducks." Although they may jump, duck, and dodge the ball, they are not allowed to catch it. If any member of the group inside the circle is hit by the ball, he or she immediately joins the players outside the circle. If the ball comes to a stop within the circle, a player inside may roll the ball back outside. If two or more players are hit with the same throw, only the first person hit joins the outside group. The last person in the middle of the circle is declared the winner. Players are reversed in the following game, with the original group inside the circle moving outside the circle and vice versa.

DODGE BALL

ALTHOUGH DODGE BALL CAN BE PLAYED IN STRAIGHT-LINE FASHION, WITH OPPOSING TEAMS FACING ONE ANOTHER ACROSS A FIELD, IT IS MORE FUN WHEN THE PLAYERS ARE CONDENSED IN AND AROUND A CIRCLE. ADJUST THE SIZE OF THE CIRCLE TO THE NUMBER OF PEOPLE PLAYING: TWO TEAMS OF FIVE SHOULD PLAY AROUND A CIRCLE AT LEAST 20 FEET IN DIAMETER. ARRANGE ONE TEAM AROUND THE OUTSIDE OF THE CIRCLE, AND THE OTHER INSIDE THE CIRCLE. THE TEAM OUTSIDE THE CIRCLE BEGINS THE GAME BY THROWING THE BALL AT THE TEAM INSIDE THE CIRCLE. IF HIT, THAT TEAM MEMBER MUST JOIN THE OPPOSING TEAM ON THE OUTSIDE. THE LAST PERSON INSIDE THE CIRCLE IS DECLARED THE WINNER. REMEMBER: TELL THE PLAYERS TO AIM THE BALL *LOW!*

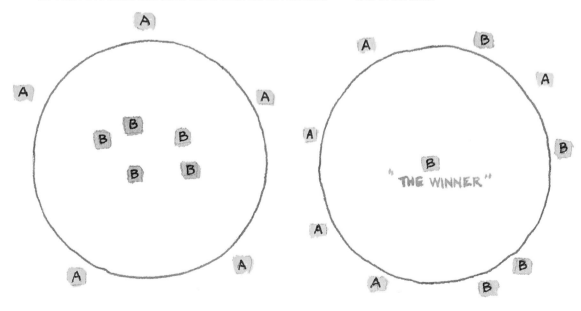

Follow the leader is a game that has been played since time immemorial. Originally played to increase a youngster's ability to follow orders for hunting and fighting, today's version has less serious implications. Implications notwithstanding, children are children, and you can bet, even long ago, there was plenty of laughter following the leader.

Follow the Leader

Follow the leader is an old-fashioned game that requires absolutely no equipment, save for the players and a leader with a good imagination. Any number of players will do, from a single follower behind the leader to a whole gang. As with most games, the more the merrier.

The name of the game—follow the leader—means exactly that: participants must go wherever the leader goes and do whatever the leader does. The object of the game is also its only rule—anyone who fails to do what the leader does is "out"—but in the action and confusion of the game, considerable leniency is usually exercised.

Begin the game by lining up the players behind the leader, about an arm's length apart. The game is then in the leader's hands, or feet, as the case may be. Hop on one leg, do a series of somersaults, swing from a tree limb, jump over a creek—you name it. A time limit may be put on each game if desired, to give everyone a chance to be the leader. And it's probably not a bad idea to caution the leader, in no uncertain terms, to keep the game safe and free of dangerous stunts.

"No one can follow me, 'cept for my dog."

Four Square

This classic school playground game can easily be played at home. All that's needed is a rubber playground ball (see page 18), some chalk to mark the court on the pavement, and four or more players.

Four square is a game where there are no clear-cut winners or losers. If there is an object, it is to advance to the server's position and stay there as long as possible, although few players seem to take much note of such a distinction.

The size of the court depends, in part, on the size of the players. Smaller players will do best on an 8- to 10-foot-square court, divided into square quarters; older, more agile players may make the court as large as 16- to 18-feet square, again divided into square quarters. Mark each quarter with a letter—A, B, C, and D—with A being the serving square.

To start the game, determine who will be the first server (see page 14). Each of the four players takes his or her place within the respective squares. The server begins play by bouncing the ball once and hitting it, usually with both hands, to any of the other quarters. The receiving player must allow the ball to bounce once before hitting it on to any other player. Play continues until someone commits a fault: stepping over the line while serving, hitting a ball on a line or outside of the court, being hit by the ball (except on the hands), or failing to hit the ball back to another player before the ball bounces a second time.

If a player commits a fault, and there are more than four players, the first person in line takes the place of the faulting player, who, in turn, takes his or her place at the end of the rotation. If there are only four players, the player who commits a fault moves to the "D" square, the server stays put, and the other two players each advance one square. If the server commits the fault, he or she moves into the "D" square and all the other players advance one square.

Fox and Geese

This old-time game is an interesting variation of tag (for other variations, see page 88). All that's needed for play is at least four players, a piece of chalk, and a paved area large enough to draw a circle 20 to 50 feet in radius.

Start by drawing the circle on the pavement. Make it as big as you want, or as big as your space will allow. If you want a nice, symmetrical circle, tie the piece of chalk to one end of a piece of twine 20 to 50 feet long. Have someone hold the chalkless end of the twine in the middle of the pavement, stretch the

FOUR SQUARE

TO PLAY THIS TRADITIONAL SCHOOL YARD GAME AT HOME, ALL YOU NEED IS SOME SIDEWALK CHALK AND A RUBBER PLAYGROUND BALL. FOR YOUNGER PLAYERS, BEGIN BY MARKING A 10-FOOT SQUARE ON THE PAVEMENT (OLDER PLAYERS MAY WANT A BIGGER PLAYING AREA, UP TO 16 OR 18 FEET SQUARE). DIVIDE THE SQUARE INTO FOUR EQUAL QUARTERS, AS SHOWN AT RIGHT, AND MARK EACH WITH A LETTER: A, B, C, AND D. "A" IS THE SERVER'S SQUARE. THIS IS A GAME OPEN TO ENDLESS VARIATIONS. YOU'LL PROBABLY FIND THAT THE YOUNGER THE PLAYER, THE MORE IT WILL VARY!

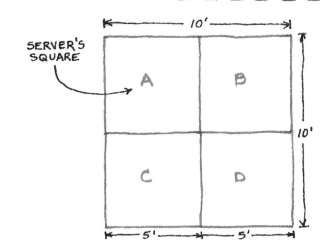

SERVER'S SQUARE

twine taut, and then make the mark by walking in a circle, keeping the twine taut the whole time. Define the inside of the circle with lines marking eight even, pie-shaped sections.

Begin the game by picking the "fox" (see page 14); the rest of the players are the "geese." The fox retreats to its den at the center of the circle, while all the geese stand on the outside line of the circle. When the signal is sounded to start the game, the fox races to try to tag the geese—with one catch: all of the players, including the fox, must stay on the lines. The first goose to be tagged by the fox, or to stumble off the lines, becomes the new fox. Play continues until exhaustion sets in.

There are many regional variations on fox and geese, including one played in a field of snow.

One less open-ended game calls for marking another circle inside the larger one. The smaller circle (which should be large enough to hold all of the geese) is the den where the fox keeps the tagged geese. Once a player has been tagged by the fox, or has stepped off any of the lines, he or she must retreat to the den in the center of the circle. In this variation, the fox wins by capturing all of the geese in the den. To make things more interesting, you can make the rule that any geese in the den can be freed by being tagged by an uncaptured goose.

Any variation of fox and geese can be played in the snow. Instead of marking the circle on the pavement, one person carefully marks the "lines" by trudging through an area of previously untrodden snow. Great winter fun!

FOX AND GEESE

FOX AND GEESE IS AN OLD-TIME VERSION OF TAG. AS MUCH FUN AS IT IS TO PLAY ON PAVEMENT, IT'S AT LEAST TWICE AS MUCH FUN WHEN PLAYED IN SNOW. EITHER WAY, START BY MARKING THE PLAYING FIELD AS SHOWN AT RIGHT. PICK WHO WILL BE THE FOX, AND THE REST OF YOU GEESE, SCRAM!

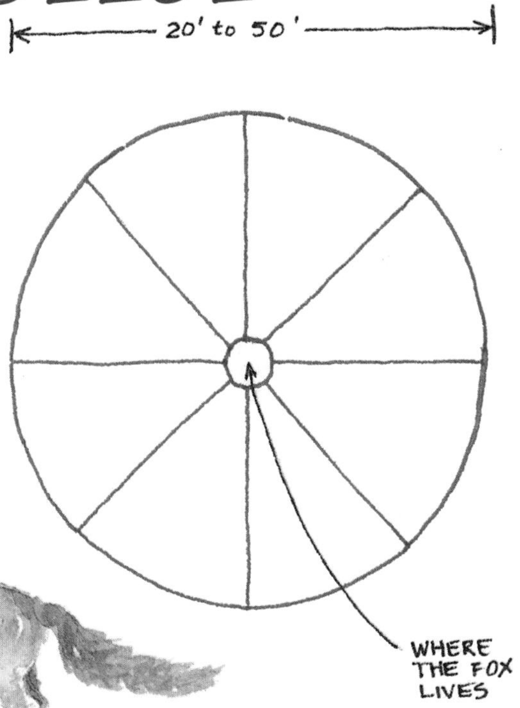

20' to 50'

WHERE THE FOX LIVES

HOPSCOTCH

SHOWN BELOW IS A DIAGRAM FOR "HEAVEN AND EARTH" HOPSCOTCH. THE INSTRUCTIONS FOR PLAY ARE TAKEN FROM *GAMES OF THE WORLD*, PUBLISHED BY UNICEF AND NOW SADLY OUT OF PRINT. THE RULES FOR HEAVEN AND EARTH HOPSCOTCH WILL APPLY TO ALMOST ANY HOPSCOTCH GAME.

A) STAND IN THE EARTH SQUARE AND TOSS YOUR MARKER INTO SQUARE #1. HOP ON ONE FOOT FROM EARTH TO SQUARE #1, PICK UP THE MARKER AND HOP BACK TO EARTH. NOW TOSS THE MARKER INTO SQUARE #2, HOP BACK TO SQUARE #2 VIA SQUARE #1, AND TOSS THE MARKER BACK TO EARTH. HOP 2, 1, THEN EARTH. BEGIN AGAIN, TOSSING THE MARKER INTO SQUARE #3, AND CONTINUE IN THE SAME MANNER UP TO SQUARE #9. IF THE MARKER LANDS IN THE WRONG BLOCK OR ON A LINE, YOUR TURN ENDS AND THE NEXT PLAYER BEGINS. (THE PLAYER WHOSE TURN IS OVER MAY BEGIN AGAIN WHERE HE OR SHE MADE THE MISTAKE, BUT ONLY AFTER THE OTHER PLAYERS HAVE TAKEN THEIR TURNS.)

B) AFTER HOPSCOTCHING FROM 1 TO 9, TOSS THE MARKER INTO HEAVEN. IF IT LANDS IN AN AREA MARKED "G," YOU MAY SKIP ONE OF THE FOLLOWING STEPS (STEPS C THROUGH K). IF THE MARKER LANDS IN HEAVEN, HOP THERE, SQUARE BY SQUARE, PICK UP THE MARKER, AND TOSS IT INTO SQUARE #9. NOW FOLLOW THE SAME PROCEDURE AS IN STEP A, BUT IN REVERSE, HOPSCOTCHING BACK TO EARTH.

C) INSTEAD OF TOSSING THE MARKER, SHOVE IT WITH YOUR FOOT FROM SQUARE TO SQUARE, AS YOU HOP FROM EARTH TO HEAVEN AND BACK TO EARTH AGAIN.

D) BALANCING THE MARKER ON ONE FOOT, HOP THROUGH ALL THE SQUARES, ONE BY ONE, TO HEAVEN AND BACK TO EARTH. IF THE MARKER FALLS OFF YOUR FOOT, YOUR TURN IS OVER.

E) DO THE SAME, BALANCING THE MARKER ON YOUR HEAD.

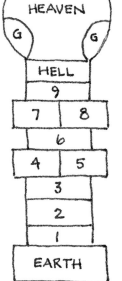

F) DO THE SAME, BALANCING THE MARKER ON YOUR INDEX FINGER.

G) DO THE SAME, BALANCING THE MARKER ON YOUR FOREARM.

H) DO THE SAME, BALANCING THE MARKER ON YOUR RIGHT KNEE.

I) DO THE SAME, BALANCING THE MARKER ON YOUR LEFT KNEE.

J) WITH EYES CLOSED AND HEAD ERECT, HOP THROUGH ALL THE SQUARES TO HEAVEN AND RETURN TO EARTH. PLAYERS CALL "HOT" AS YOU HOP CORRECTLY, "COLD" IF YOU MISS.

K) STANDING IN EARTH, WITH YOUR BACK TOWARD THE HOPSCOTCH DIAGRAM, TOSS THE MARKER OVER YOUR SHOULDER. IF THE MARKER FALLS INTO ONE OF THE SQUARES AND NOT ON A LINE, YOU MAY WRITE YOUR INITIALS ON THE SQUARE, MAKING IT YOUR "HOUSE." IN SUBSEQUENT GAMES, YOU MAY REST THERE WITH BOTH FEET ON THE GROUND. THE OTHER PLAYERS MUST SKIP THIS BLOCK WHEN PLAYING.

GENERAL RULES

1) WHILE RESTING IN HEAVEN, YOU MAY STAND ON BOTH FEET AND READJUST THE POSITION OF A BADLY PLACED MARKER.

2) IF YOUR MARKER LANDS ON A LINE OR IN THE WRONG SQUARE, YOU LOSE YOUR TURN.

3) IF THE MARKER LANDS IN THE POST SECTION OF HEAVEN, YOU MAY NOT SPEAK OR LAUGH DURING THE GAME, OR YOU ARE OUT OF THE GAME FOR GOOD.

4) IF THE MARKER LANDS IN THE HELL SECTION OF HEAVEN, YOU END YOUR TURN AND MUST START FROM THE BEGINNING WHEN YOUR TURN COMES UP AGAIN.

Hopscotch

Hopscotch is one of the oldest, most widely played games in the world. From Britain to Burma, from Russia to India, across oceans and cultures, to America and back to Europe—there are hopscotch patterns scratched in sand, painted on playgrounds, or marked on the sidewalk with charcoal or chalk. Although there are countless variations, what surprises researchers is not the differences in hopscotch from one country to another, but the similarities. And in case you were wondering, the name "hopscotch" doesn't relate in any way to Scotland. The word "scotch" is an old English word that means to "mark lightly," relating to the way the hopscotch diagram is marked lightly onto the pavement or other surface.

We know the ancient Romans played hopscotch, because about 2,000 years ago, someone cut a hopscotch pattern into the stone floor of the forum in Rome. As the Roman legions marched into Europe and Britain, they built roads and, among other activities, played hopscotch on those roads, teaching youngsters the game along the way. Some of these ancient hopscotch courses were more than 100 feet long. It has been suggested that in addition to being a game, hopscotch was a means for soldiers of ancient times to increase their strength and agility by working their way through the hopscotch patterns while laden with backpacks and other heavy supplies.

The object of hopscotch is the same no matter where it is played: to navigate through the hopscotch pattern in the right sequence, using the correct steps, without stepping on a line or having your marker land on a line.

You'll need something with which to draw the hopscotch diagram, such as chalk for the sidewalk or a stick if you're

"I always keep my favorite rock in my pocket just in case I want to play hopscotch at recess."

playing on the sand, and a small something to use as your marker. Markers can be anything—an empty shoe polish tin filled with sand (an object known as a "potsie"), a little sand-filled fabric pouch (like a small beanbag), or simply a special stone picked up from a gravel pile.

H-O-R-S-E

If you want to play some basketball, but there aren't enough players around to make a team, horse is the game you want to play. No one seems to know the origins of horse, but it has been played for generations, from one end of this country to the other. It's a lot of fun to play, and in its own way contains the essence of competitive play.

To play horse, you'll need a basketball goal, a basketball, and at least two players. Decide who goes first by shooting free throws (the first person to sink a free throw goes first), or by one of the methods described on page 14.

Whoever is first begins the game by attempting to make a basket, the more difficult the shot the better. If the first contestant successfully makes the shot, the second contestant must repeat it, identically. If unsuccessful in his or her attempt, the second contestant is saddled with an "H," the first letter of horse. If successful in repeating the shot, the second contestant then performs his or her own shot, which the first contestant must then imitate.

The first person to spell out all the letters in horse, loses the game . . . maybe. There is a variation of horse, called "saved at the line," that allows the first person to earn an "E" to erase it by successfully making a free throw. Something like a last minute reprieve, "saved at the line" adds an interesting twist to the game, while allowing it to continue past its usual conclusion.

In a horse game with more than two players, play as above. If the first player makes a basket, and the second player is successful in repeating it, the

You don't need a horse to play h-o-r-s-e, but you may be the horse if you don't make the basket.

third player is also required to try to make the same shot. If, however, the second player fails in duplicating the shot, the third player starts fresh, attempting a basket in whatever style he or she chooses.

Horseshoes

That old line—"close only counts in horseshoes and hand grenades"—isn't altogether true. Close also counts in bocce, jeu de boules, lawn bowls, and a few other games here and there. Regardless of the accuracy of the statement, it indicates that horseshoes is a game where precision isn't everything.

The game of horseshoes dates back to a similar game played by soldiers in ancient Rome. When the Romans conquered Britain, they took the game with them. From Britain, the game of horseshoes crossed the ocean to America with the early settlers and has been played in this country ever since.

The game was originally played with standard horseshoes (the type used to shoe horses). Since the 1920s, special "open shoes" have replaced the standard horseshoe as the favored shoe for pitching. This is the type sold in horseshoe kits at sporting goods stores. The National Horseshoe Pitchers Associa-

tion defines an official horseshoe as follows: "A shoe shall not exceed 7¼ inches in width, 7⅝ inches in length, and shall not weigh more than 2 pounds, 10 ounces. On a parallel line three-quarters of an inch from a straight edge touching the points of the open end of a shoe, the opening shall not exceed 3½ inches. Where all measurements are specified as maximum, there is no minimum." That ought to clear up any confusion.

The object of the game is to pitch the horseshoes so they are caught by the stake—a feat known as a "ringer." In addition to ringers, horseshoes six inches or closer to the stake are counted in a player's score (for the official method of scoring points, see page 107). The first person or team to reach 40 points wins the game. Tournament play usually requires the individual player or team to win the best two out of three, or the best three out of five games.

An official horseshoe court requires a space 6 by 50 feet (see diamgram below). Although it seems like a large area, many suburban lots can accommodate a horseshoe court in a side yard—an underused space if there ever was one.

The official rules for horseshoes, as put forth by the National Horseshoe Pitchers Association of America, can be found on page 107.

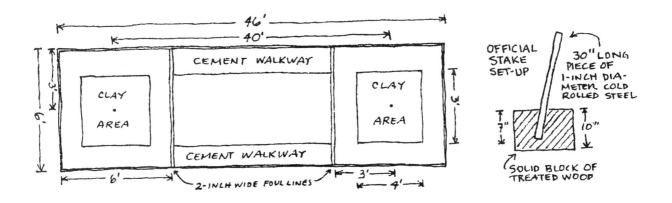

*The game of jacks, in a much
earlier variation, used to be
played to foretell the future.
Today, the game is played just for
fun, but it's still just as hard to
play jacks well as it is to predict
what tomorrow will bring.*

Jacks

Jacks is played with a set of ten "jacks" (small star shapes made of metal) and a rubber ball. In ancient Greece a similar game (minus the ball) was played with the dried knucklebones from sheep. The knucklebones looked similar to modern dice.

The ancient Greeks took their games with them on their conquests, spreading the game's popularity. The Romans, in turn, adopted many of the ancient Greek pastimes and spread their popularity during their far-flung exploits. That said, it's interesting to note that games almost identical to "knucklebones" have been played for eons in parts of the world the ancient Greeks and Romans didn't even know existed. Whether the game is called jacks, fivestones, knucklebones, checkstones, or is played in Polynesia, Russia, England, or America, the similarity between the games and the enjoyment they provide indicate a universal, timeless appeal.

Jacks is a game that can be played alone, with two persons, or occasionally more. It is most popularly played between two people.

To play the modern American version of jacks, all that is needed is a set of jacks, a small rubber ball (one friend related that, as a child, she often substituted a Ping-Pong ball when the rubber ball couldn't be found), and a smooth surface, such as a schoolyard, an uncarpeted floor, or a sidewalk or patio.

Although there are many variations, winning usually means picking up all the jacks, one at a time, in between bounces of the ball.

"I have an uncle named Jack. I think this game is named after him."

JACKS

PICTURED HERE IS A VERY OLD VARIATION OF JACKS CALLED "FIRST JACK," FOUND IN THE 1901 EDITION OF *THE OUTDOOR HANDY BOOK:*

THE GAME OPENS WITH ONE PLAYER TAKING THE FIVE JACKS IN HIS OR HER HAND. HOLDING THE HAND, PALM UP (1),

(2) THE JACKS ARE TOSSED INTO THE AIR

(3) BEFORE THE JACKS HAVE TIME TO DESCEND, THE PLAYER TURNS HIS OR HER HAND OVER AND CATCHES AS MANY AS POSSIBLE ON THE BACK OF THE HAND

THESE ARE AGAIN TOSSED UP (4), AND BEFORE THEY DESCEND, THE PLAYER PICKS UP THOSE JACKS WHICH HE OR SHE FAILED TO CATCH ON THE BACK OF HIS OR HER HAND (5).

QUICKLY TURNING THE HAND, THE PLAYERS CATCHES THE DESCENDING JACKS, AND HOLDS ALL OF THEM (6).

WHENEVER A PLAYER FAILS, THE NEXT IN LINE TAKES THE JACKS.

Begin the game by tossing all of the jacks into the air, turning your hand over (back side up), and catching as many jacks as you can on the back of your hand. The person who catches the most jacks starts the play.

The first player scatters all of the jacks on the ground. He or she then throws the ball into the air, allows it to bounce once (in most variations of the game), then picks up a single jack (without disturbing any of its neighbors), catching the ball before it has a chance to bounce a second time.

If this first try is successful, the player continues to bounce the ball and pick up a single jack at a time, keeping all of the accumulated jacks in his or her hand through the course of the game. If the first player ever fails to pick up a jack or catch the ball or disturbs a neighboring jack, the turn goes to the next player, who starts a new game by tossing all of the jacks on the ground.

The first person to successfully pick up all of the jacks is the winner.

Variations: One of the simplest variations, good for beginning jacks players, involves changing the one-bounce rule to two bounces.

One of the most popular (and difficult) variations is to increase by one the number of jacks you pick up with each successive bounce of the ball. On your first try you pick up one jack, second try, two jacks, third try, three jacks, and so forth until all the jacks are removed from the field of play.

Another variation, called "eggs in the basket" in some neighborhoods, involves tossing the picked-up jack to your opposite hand before catching the ball.

Popular in Europe are several variations where an arch (formed with the thumb and forefinger) or "stable" (formed with all fingers outstretched like a spider) is made near the jacks. When the ball is tossed in the air, the player flicks one jack at a time under the arch or into the stable before catching the ball after its first bounce.

The first person with all of his or her jacks under the arch or in the stable wins.

Jeu de Boules

If you have ever been to France, for even a short stay, then you probably have encountered the familiar sight of a passionate game of boules in progress on any number of public or private courts. Boules is an extremely popular game throughout France, especially with retirees.

The game has its roots in ancient Greece. It was there that men in their "senior years" began taking their exercise by throwing various-sized balls as far as possible. The ancient Romans adopted the practice, but added a target as something to aim for. As the Roman Empire expanded, so did the popularity of what we now call jeu de boules.

The most popular games, worldwide, seem to be those that combine simplicity of rules with maximum regard for skillful strategy and a minimum emphasis on superhuman strength or luck. This would explain the enormous popularity (bordering on fanaticism) of jeu de boules and its close Italian cousin, bocce (see page 29).

Although neither boules nor bocce has gained widespread popularity in America, it may only be a matter of time. One French writer observed that boules players (known in France as *boulistes*) hit their prime between the ages of 40 and 50 years old, when the players have gained enough life experience to know the value of patience and strategy, but before time takes its toll on physical strength. With America's population staying in better shape and living longer, who knows? Perhaps we'll begin seeing the emergence of jeu de boules courts in parks, town squares, and private gardens.

In France, jeu de boules is played with specially manufactured iron balls, approximately four inches in diameter, and the much smaller target ball (usually made of wood), called a *cochonnet*. Lacking these, croquet balls make an acceptable substitute for throwing, and a golf ball stands in nicely as a *cochonnet*.

An official boules court is 3 by 27.5 meters (approximately 9 feet, 9 inches by 89 feet, 9 inches), but considerable leniency is allowed. In common practice, the length of the court is determined by how far the players can throw the ball. Almost all courts one sees are constructed of hard-packed dirt, leveled, and edged with a low curb of wood or concrete.

"Jeu de boules? I think we had it for dinner last night. It was awful."

JEU DE BOULES

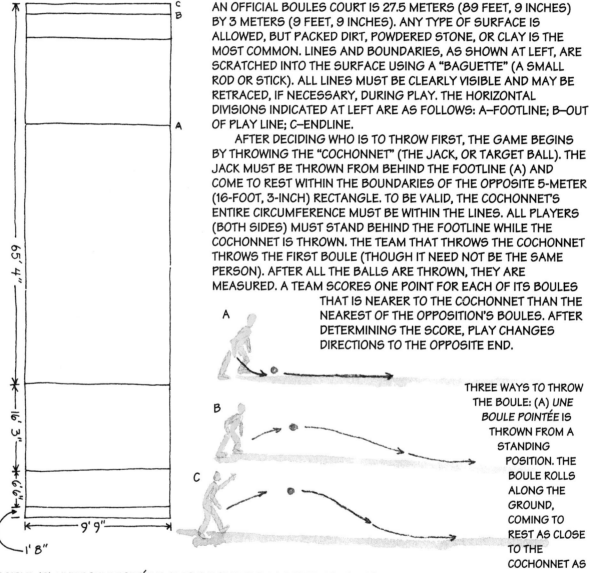

AN OFFICIAL BOULES COURT IS 27.5 METERS (89 FEET, 9 INCHES) BY 3 METERS (9 FEET, 9 INCHES). ANY TYPE OF SURFACE IS ALLOWED, BUT PACKED DIRT, POWDERED STONE, OR CLAY IS THE MOST COMMON. LINES AND BOUNDARIES, AS SHOWN AT LEFT, ARE SCRATCHED INTO THE SURFACE USING A "BAGUETTE" (A SMALL ROD OR STICK). ALL LINES MUST BE CLEARLY VISIBLE AND MAY BE RETRACED, IF NECESSARY, DURING PLAY. THE HORIZONTAL DIVISIONS INDICATED AT LEFT ARE AS FOLLOWS: A—FOOTLINE; B—OUT OF PLAY LINE; C—ENDLINE.

AFTER DECIDING WHO IS TO THROW FIRST, THE GAME BEGINS BY THROWING THE "COCHONNET" (THE JACK, OR TARGET BALL). THE JACK MUST BE THROWN FROM BEHIND THE FOOTLINE (A) AND COME TO REST WITHIN THE BOUNDARIES OF THE OPPOSITE 5-METER (16-FOOT, 3-INCH) RECTANGLE. TO BE VALID, THE COCHONNET'S ENTIRE CIRCUMFERENCE MUST BE WITHIN THE LINES. ALL PLAYERS (BOTH SIDES) MUST STAND BEHIND THE FOOTLINE WHILE THE COCHONNET IS THROWN. THE TEAM THAT THROWS THE COCHONNET THROWS THE FIRST BOULE (THOUGH IT NEED NOT BE THE SAME PERSON). AFTER ALL THE BALLS ARE THROWN, THEY ARE MEASURED. A TEAM SCORES ONE POINT FOR EACH OF ITS BOULES THAT IS NEARER TO THE COCHONNET THAN THE NEAREST OF THE OPPOSITION'S BOULES. AFTER DETERMINING THE SCORE, PLAY CHANGES DIRECTIONS TO THE OPPOSITE END.

THREE WAYS TO THROW THE BOULE: (A) *UNE BOULE POINTÉE* IS THROWN FROM A STANDING POSITION. THE BOULE ROLLS ALONG THE GROUND, COMING TO REST AS CLOSE TO THE COCHONNET AS POSSIBLE; (B) *UNE BOULE PORTÉE* IS ALSO THROWN FROM A STANDING POSITION, BUT THE BOULE TRAVELS IN AN ARC THROUGH THE AIR, COMING TO REST AS CLOSE TO THE COCHONNET AS POSSIBLE; (C) *UNE BOULE TIRÉE* IS THROWN ON A RUN; SOLELY INTENDED TO HIT AND DISPLACE THE COCHONNNET OR AN OPPONENT'S BOULE.

A minimum of two players is needed to play, but two teams of two, three, or four (at the most), is more common. If team play is what you're after, it's a good idea for each team to have different-colored balls and for teammates to mark their names on their balls. If only two people are playing, each player receives three or four balls; for team play, with two or more players per side, each player receives two balls.

As with bocce, the object of the game is to throw as many of your balls (or your team's balls) as close to the cochonnet as possible.

Begin the game by tossing a coin to see who will throw the cochonnet into position. The cochonnet thrower then positions him or herself at one end of the court, scratches a footline in the dirt and throws the cochonnet. To qualify as a "live" target, the cochonnet must come to rest in the opposite 16 foot, 3 inch rectangle. If, as in many improvised boules courts, there are obstacles in the playing field (such as a bush or a rock), the cochonnet must land a minimum of 20 inches from any such obstacle. If the cochonnet lands in an unacceptable zone, the same thrower repeats the process until the cochonnet is valid.

Once the cochonnet is in position, the same thrower begins the competition by throwing a ball as close to the cochonnet as possible. See the illustration on page 52 for three ways to deliver the ball: *boule pointée, boule portée,* and *boule tirée.*

Interestingly (and this is where strategy comes into play), it is okay if the thrown ball hits the cochonnet and knocks it from its original position. As the French say: *"Le cochonnet est là où il est"* (the target is where the target is).

After the first ball has been thrown, the next throw belongs to the opposing team. Thereafter, whichever team has a ball closest to the target cedes the next throw to the opposition. Players throw only one ball per turn.

If one team throws the last of its balls without coming closest to the target, the opposing team is allowed to throw the remainder of its balls, consecutively.

An individual game is over when all the balls have been thrown. The team with a ball closest to the target is declared the winner. The winning team receives one point for each of its balls that lie closer to the target than the closest ball of the opposing team. The winning team throws the cochonnet for the next game. Traditionally, subsequent tosses of the cochon-

Do you know what the word "cochonnet" means in French? Somewhat mysteriously, it means "little pig." Now why, you might ask, would the French call a small target ball a little pig? Good question. Almost as good as why Americans call their toes "little pigs"—as in "this little piggy went to market, this little piggy stayed home..." Mysterious, indeed.

net take place from its final resting place in the previous game. A "round" of games (and its winner) is declared when the first team reaches either 13 or 15 points (a score decided upon in advance).

If you've ever had the opportunity to watch a boules game in full swing, you realize that rolling the ball down the court is only one option, and a fairly tame one at that. In trying to knock an opponent's ball away from the cochonnet, most experienced players will opt for throwing their ball through the air *(une boule tiree)* hoping for a direct hit. The reasoning behind this is not just to show off, but to avoid some of the pitfalls of rolling a ball down a court that, more often than not, is strewn with pebbles, divots, or roots. A straight course through thin air may not have the same obstacles, but scoring direct hits on an opposing team's ball takes considerable practice and expertise.

Jeu de boules is played virtually everywhere in France. Generally it's the older generation who takes the game most seriously (perhaps because they are the ones with the time to devote to its subtleties), but people of all ages turn out to witness a particularly exciting match. As with bocce, the appeal is in the infinite refinements of an essentially simple game.

Kickball

This is an easy game to play, particularly well suited for kids in the lower elementary grades.

You'll need at least six players, a rubber playground ball, and a large outdoor area. Set up the playing field like a baseball diamond, with first, second, and third bases and home plate clearly marked, each approximately 25 to 30 feet apart.

Divide the group into two teams. Decide who will be first up (see page 14) and have them line up in "kicking order." The team in the field should take positions similar to baseball—first, second, and third base, left, right, and center fielder, catcher and pitcher—filling as many of the positions as you can with the number of players available. If there aren't enough players to fill all the positions, the game may still be played successfully.

The pitcher stands 15 or so feet away from home plate, rolling the ball to the kicker (as I recall, at my elementary school, we actually requested the way we wanted the ball delivered, with "slow and bouncy" being the favorite). The kicker kicks the ball as hard as he or she can and runs the bases, as in baseball.

Once a ball has been kicked and is in play, there are three ways for the opposing team to declare the runner out: 1) catch the kicked ball on the fly, without it having bounced first; 2) tag first base with the ball before the runner has a chance to reach the base; 3) touch the runner with the ball—either by tagging or throwing—while the runner is not on a base. (Establish before the game that balls thrown at the head do not count as "outs.")

"I love this game. Just give it to me slow and bouncy, and I'll kick it over the fence."

One of the reasons this is such a popular game with youngsters is that, given such a large ball, it's fairly hard not to score a "hit."

Even so, balls kicked at and simply missed are counted as strikes (three strikes and the kicker is out), as are the first two "foul" balls kicked. If a third foul ball is kicked, however, it does not count as the final strike; the kicker simply continues to try to score a hit.

As in baseball, three outs constitute half an inning, at which point the teams trade places. Both sides should decide ahead of time how many innings the game will last. The team with the most runs in at the end of the game wins.

KICKBALL

IT IS EASIEST TO THINK OF A KICKBALL FIELD AS A VARIATION OF A BASEBALL DIAMOND: HOME PLATE AND FIRST, SECOND, AND THIRD BASES ARE ALL IN THE SAME POSITION AS BASEBALL, WITH APROXIMATELY 25 TO 30 FEET BETWEEN EACH BASE. THE "PITCHER'S MOUND" SHOULD BE APPROXIMATELY 15 FEET FROM HOME PLATE.

THE TYPE OF BALL USED FOR KICKBALL IS SOMEWHAT DETERMINED BY THE AGE OF THE PLAYERS. USE A RUBBER PLAYGROUND BALL FOR YOUNGSTERS; A HARDER, SMALLER BALL IS APPROPRIATE FOR OLDER PLAYERS.

AS IN BASEBALL, THREE OUTS MAKE HALF AN INNING IN KICKBALL. AFTER THE THIRD OUT, TEAMS TRADE PLACES ON THE FIELD. BOTH SIDES SHOULD DECIDE AHEAD OF TIME HOW MANY INNINGS THE GAME WILL LAST. THE TEAM WITH THE MOST RUNS WINS.

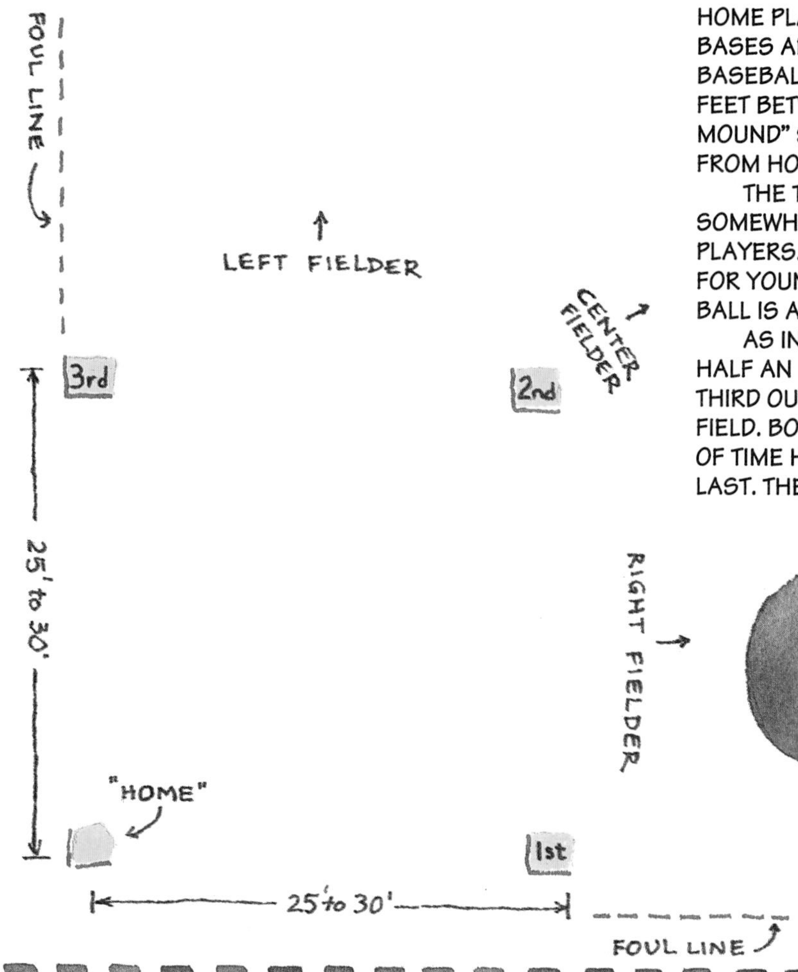

FOUL LINE

LEFT FIELDER

CENTER FIELDER

3rd

2nd

25' to 30'

RIGHT FIELDER

A RUBBER PLAYGROUND BALL MAKES A SUITABLE KICKBALL FOR PLAYERS IN THE "JUNIOR LEAGUE."

"HOME"

1st

25' to 30'

FOUL LINE

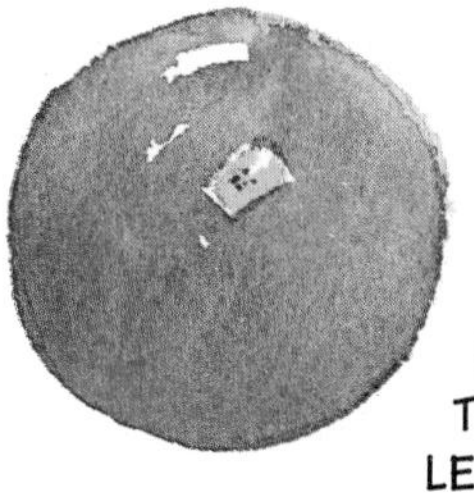

Lawn Bowls

Lawn bowls is very similar to both the French jeu de boules and Italy's bocce; in fact, all three share a common ancestry in ancient Greek and Roman ball games. All three involve rolling large balls as close as possible to a smaller target ball, all three have similar scoring systems and rules, and the players of all three games do so with such enthusiasm, all have been labeled "fanatics" at one time or another.

What sets lawn bowls apart from jeu de boules and bocce, however, is the fact that it is played on a lawn—and a mighty fine, mighty large one at that. You know how fine a golf course putting green is? Well, just imagine a putting green approximately 132 feet square, and you get an idea of what sets lawn bowls apart from boules and bocce, both of which are played on some fairly rough-and-tumble, packed dirt courts. Official lawn bowl courts, called "greens," are surrounded by a two-inch-deep ditch. Another feature unique to lawn bowls is the fact that the balls (called bowls) are slightly oblique, which causes them to roll in a curved rather than a straight line. Be that as it may, it's the lawn, rather than the balls, that really sets this game apart from its close cousins, boules and bocce.

The sheer size of the green, not to mention the maintenance it requires, takes lawn bowls out of the "backyard" game category: Let's face it, anyone with a regulation lawn bowls court in his or her backyard probably wouldn't call the backyard a backyard. The game is included here because there's nothing stopping people from playing lawn bowls by their own set of rules, on whatever kind or size of lawn they might have.

Aside from a lawn, you'll need a set of lawn bowls to play this game. Sets of lawn bowls (there are four in a set) come in

"I don't understand. What kind of a game do you play with bowls on the lawn?"

LAWN BOWLS

THE TRADITIONAL SERIES OF LAWN BOWL RINKS (EACH APPROXIMATELY 19 FEET WIDE BY 132 FEET LONG) IS DIFFICULT TO ACCOMMODATE IN MOST BACKYARDS. LACKING THE SPACE FOR AN OFFICIAL SERIES OF RINKS, ONE MIGHT OPT FOR A SINGLE RINK—A MORE LIKELY POSSIBILITY, ESPECIALLY IF A LONG, NARROW SIDE YARD IS INCORPORATED AS PART OF THE PLAYING FIELD. THEN THERE IS THE QUESTION OF THE GRASS THAT COVERS A LAWN BOWLS RINK, WHICH SHOULD BE VERY FINE AND PERFECTLY LEVEL. WELL, WHERE THERE'S A WILL (OR A GOOD-SIZED TRUST FUND), THERE'S A WAY …

LAWN BOWLS IS VERY CLOSELY RELATED TO BOTH THE ITALIAN BOCCE (PAGE 29) AND THE FRENCH JEU DE BOULES (PAGE 51). THAT LAWN BOWLS IS AN ENGLISH GAME, HOWEVER, HAS RESULTED IN AN EVEN MORE PRESCRIBED ORDER OF PLAY, A STRICT CODE OF CONDUCT, AND, OF COURSE, A STRONGLY RECOMMENDED DRESS CODE, NOT TO MENTION ITS OWN, PECULIAR TERMINOLOGY. BE A GOOD SPORT AND MIND YOUR MANNERS, PLEASE!

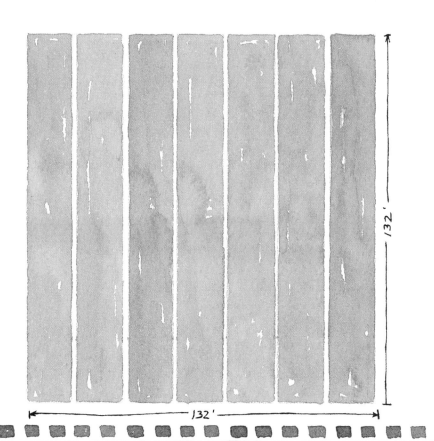

eight sizes (numbered from 0 to 7) designed for different-size players. Each size is available in heavy and medium weight. There are two rules of thumb for choosing the size and weight of the bowl: spread your two hands around the ball. If your thumbs and middle fingers just touch, the bowl should be the right size. Once you've picked the right-size bowl, determine whether you need a heavy- or medium-weight bowl by holding the bowl upside down in your hand. Slap the top of your hand with your free hand. If the bowl falls out, opt for the lighter weight model. Official bowls may not exceed 3½ pounds in weight or 5⅛ inches in diameter. Each ball has a marking that's unique to that set of four balls; in this way, you can distinguish your balls from someone else's.

In addition to a place to play and your own set of four bowls, you also need a jack (the little white target ball), one regulation mat, and a pair of flat, rubber-soled shoes (especially if you are playing on an official green).

You win at lawn bowls by getting more of your (or your team's) bowls near the jack than your opponent(s).

Lawn bowls can be played with two, four, six, or eight people. A two-person game (one playing against the other) is known as singles; each person has four bowls with which to play. Pairs, or doubles, consists of opposing teams of two people. As with singles, pairs play with four bowls per person. Triples (three people to a team) play with three bowls per person, and rinks, or fours (four people to a team), play with two bowls per person.

For individual games, the green is usually divided into seven or eight courts called "rinks" (14 to 19 feet wide by 132 feet long), separated from one another by a green cord.

The official rules for lawn bowls, as set forth by the American Lawn Bowls Association, can be found on page 109. Although every game has its own unique terminology, lawn bowls seems to have more than its fair share. The following are a few definitions for lawn bowling terms that should help you understand the official rules:

End: Baseball has innings. Football has quarters. Hockey has periods. Lawn bowls has ends. An end is completed when all players on both sides have delivered their bowls in one direction on the green. A game consists of a predetermined number of ends, usually between 18 and 21.

Jack: The small ball, thrown first and used as a target for the larger bowls, known in parts of Britain as a "cot" or "kitty."

"I get it now, but why won't my ball roll straight?"

Green: The perfectly level, grass playing field on which seven or eight lawn bowls games may be played simultaneously. International competitions stipulate that the green be a minimum of 120 feet square. The entire green is surrounded by a two-inch-deep ditch.

Lead: See "teammate duties."

Mat: Official mats are 14 inches wide by 24 inches long, made of black rubber with a two-inch white border (also called a "footer"). At the start of game, the mat is centered, with its front edge six feet from the rear ditch. At the moment a ball or jack is released from a player's hand, one of the player's feet must be completely on or above the mat.

Rink: A part of the green, approximately 19 by 132 feet, on which individual games of lawn bowls are played.

Skip: See "teammate duties."

Toucher: A bowl that touches the jack.

Teammate duties: In a three-person team, each person is assigned a job. The lead centers the mat and throws the jack, thereby beginning the game. The skip is the team captain and acts as director, deciding disputes with opponents. In pairs or doubles, the skip also carries the scorecard. The vice-skip acts as director when the skip is playing, makes any necessary measurements, and determines with his or her opponent the results of an end. In a triples match, the vice-skip carries the scorecard.

Vice-skip: See "teammate duties."

Leapfrog

Just about everyone knows how to leapfrog over another person, but few have witnessed a real leapfrog race between two opposing teams. It's quite a sight.

You'll need at least six people (more is better, and there's no real limit) divided into even teams, a large lawn, and a way to mark the start and finish lines.

Line up the teams behind the starting line. Before the race begins, the first person in each line walks about 10 or 15 paces in front of the starting line and settles into the "frog" position—knees bent, arms folded under the knees and, most important of all, *head down.* At the sound of the start, the second person in line gets a running start and then leaps over

Remember, keep your head down when the frog is leaping over you: It improves the frog's time and keeps your head from getting bonked.

60

the frog by placing his or her hands of the back of the frog, spreading his or her legs, and catapulting over. Once over, the leaper assumes the frog position, five feet or so in front of the first frog. As soon as the second frog is in position, the third person in line repeats the process, jumping over each frog.

When the last person in line has jumped over all the frogs and is in the frog position at the head of the line, the original frog (now at the tail end of the frog line) leaps over all the frogs in front of him or her and then races toward the finish line. As soon as the frog at the back of the line has been jumped over, that person gets up and begins leaping over the frogs in front of him or her—and so on, the whole spectacle looking a little like a human carpet being rolled up before your very eyes. The first team with all its leapfrogs over the finish line wins.

London Bridge

The name of this game is taken from the famous London Bridge in London, England—originally built of wood during ancient Roman occupation of the area, and replaced between the years 1176 and 1209 with a stone bridge under the direction of Peter of Colechurch. The old London Bridge remained the only bridge spanning the river Thames for almost 600 years, until the 1740s, when the Westminster Bridge was built farther down the river. The actual London Bridge is thought to have originated as the result of the many calamities that struck the original wooden bridge over a long period of time, such as fires, floods, and wartime destruction.

Bridges are commonplace today, but in much earlier cultures they were looked upon with a combination of awe and suspicion. As with almost all technological advances, such as the airplane or skyscraper of more modern times, a fair degree of fear and skepticism accompanied their introduction. In earlier times (and perhaps even today), there was the lingering suspicion that perhaps man had gone too far, and the gods would seek retribution for such a lack of humility and respect. This appears to be a universal human response, for, in addition to the London Bridge game, many "fallen bridge" games are found in other parts of the world—Scotland (Broken Bridges), Germany (*Die Goldene Brücke*), and France (*Le Pont-Levis*)—

"The London Bridge part is okay, but I like the tug-of-war part best."

61

all of which date to roughly the same time.

There should be at least eight players, although there's no limit. Two act as the "bridge keepers." The bridge keepers stand facing each other, clasp each other's hands, and raise their arms high to form an arch. The players are instructed to line up, hold on to each other's waists, and pass under the arch, all the while singing the London Bridge song. The traditional verses are as follows (don't be surprised is they don't jibe with the ones you were taught as a child—there are countless variations).

London Bridge Is Falling Down

London Bridge is falling down,
Falling down, falling down,
London Bridge is falling down,
My fair lady.

How shall we build it up again,
Up again, up again,
How shall we build it up again,
My fair lady.

We will build it of wood and clay,
Wood and clay, wood and clay,
We will build it of wood and clay,
My fair lady.

But wood and clay will wash away,
Wash away, wash away,
But wood and clay will wash away,
My fair lady.

We will build it of iron and steel,
Iron and steel, iron and steel,
We will build it of iron and steel,
My fair lady.

But iron and steel will break away,
Break away, break away,
But iron and steel will break away,
My fair lady.

We will build it of silver and gold,
Silver and gold, silver and gold,
We will build it of silver and gold,
My fair lady.

But silver and gold will be stolen away,
Stolen away, stolen away,
But silver and gold will be stolen away,
My fair lady.

We will put a man to watch all night,
Watch all night, watch all night,
We will put a man to watch all night,
My fair lady.

Suppose the man should fall asleep,
Fall asleep, fall asleep,
Suppose the man should fall asleep,
My fair lady.

Take the keys and lock him up,
Lock him up, lock him up,
Take the keys and lock him up,
My fair lady.

At the sound of the next to last line—"take the keys and lock him up"—the bridge keepers quickly lower their arms, capturing one of the players in the process.

In one version of the game, the captured players are taken to the Tower of London, where they must remain until all the players have been captured and imprisoned. Once the last player is taken to the Tower, the captors set all the players free in one fell swoop and chase them around the yard. The first two tagged become the next bridge keepers.

Another version of the game has the bridge keepers ask the captives, as they are being taken to the Tower of London, what they would rather be: cabbages or roses? Or sometimes the choice of gold or silver is given. When all of the players are finally imprisoned in the Tower, the bridge keepers divide the group into cabbages and roses, or what have you, and assemble a tug-of-war (see page 92) between the two sides. Interestingly, this variation has its roots in the Medieval belief that good and evil were represented by the two sides of a bridge. Tug-of-war games in almost every culture around the world seem to embody this struggle between good and evil.

Did you know that if the London Bridge falls on you, you have to go to the Tower of London and stay there until your captors set you free? And after everyone has been locked in the tower, a tug-of-war must be played? This game is not all that it appears to be!

MARBLES

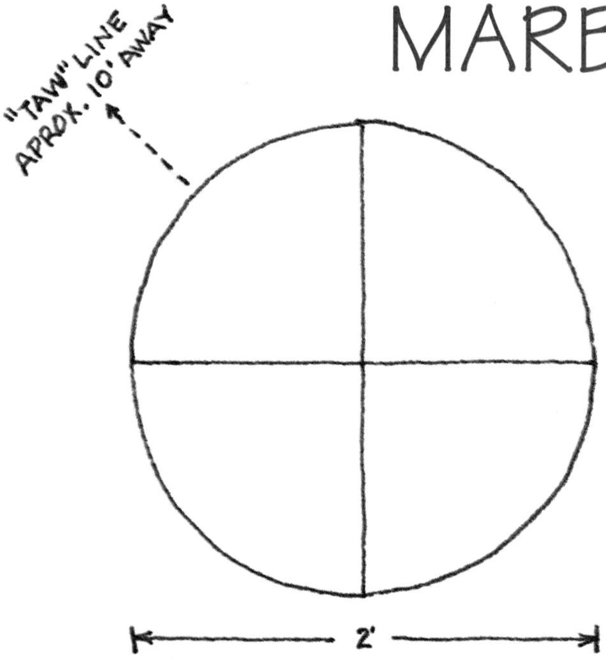

2'

ILLUSTRATED AT LEFT IS A RING FOR PLAYING AN OLD-FASHIONED VERSION OF MARBLES CALLED "YANK," SUITABLE FOR ANY NUMBER OF PLAYERS. IF ONLY TWO PLAY, EACH PLACES ONE MARBLE IN THE RING; ONE ON THE RIGHT SIDE, AND THE OTHER ON THE LEFT. IF MORE THAN TWO PLAY, ARRANGE A MARBLE FROM EACH PLAYER EVENLY AROUND THE CIRCLE. THE FIRST PERSON TO PLAY SCRATCHES A "TAW" LINE ABOUT 10 FEET FROM THE CIRCLE. IT IS FROM THE TAW LINE THAT THE PLAYER PLACES HIS OR HER KNUCKLE DABSTER (SEE BELOW), "KNUCKLES DOWN," AND SHOOTS AT THE MARBLES. IF THE PLAYER KNOCKS A MARBLE OUT OF THE CIRCLE, HE OR SHE POCKETS THE MARBLE AND TAKES ANOTHER TURN, PLAYING FROM WHERE THE SHOOTER HAS COME TO REST. IF MISSED, THE NEXT PLAYER TAKES A TURN. IF PLAYER #2 HITS PLAYER #1'S SHOOTER, HE OR SHE NOT ONLY POCKETS THAT MARBLE, BUT ALL THE MARBLES PLAYER #1 HAS PREVIOUSLY WON. IF THERE ARE ONLY TWO PLAYERS, AND ONE OF THE MARBLES IS KNOCKED OUT, THE OWNER MUST REPLACE IT WITH A NEW ONE.

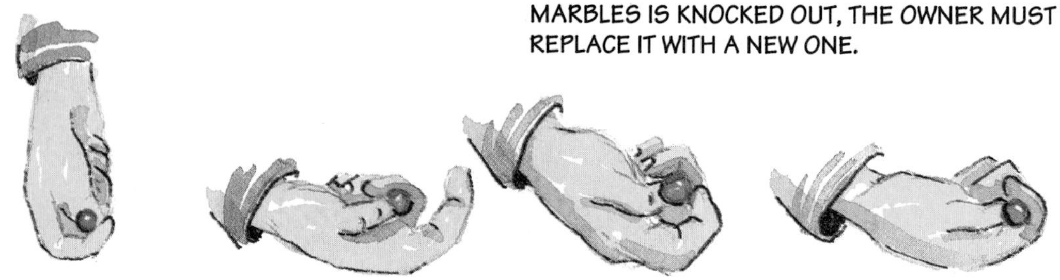

FOUR WAYS TO SHOOT: A) SCRUMPY KNUCKLED, B)THE HUCK FINN, C) NEW YORK, D) THE PREFERRED "PRO."

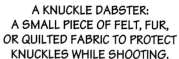

ACS
1992

A KNUCKLE DABSTER:
A SMALL PIECE OF FELT, FUR,
OR QUILTED FABRIC TO PROTECT
KNUCKLES WHILE SHOOTING.

IF YOU GET INTO MARBLES IN A BIG WAY,
MAKE YOURSELF A MARBLE BAG FROM A PIECE CANVAS.
A DRAWSTRING TOP PROTECTS YOUR AGGIES, CLEARIES,
AND STEELIES FROM GETTING LOST.

Marbles

Judging by the recent availability of beautiful marbles, it appears that the game is once again rising in popularity. Marbles, in and of themselves, are wonderful to collect: even better is to use them for play, and perhaps add some of your opponent's marbles to your own collection.

Although there are many variations, the object of the most common form of the game is to knock an opponent's marbles out of a circle. In tournament play, the circle is ten feet in diameter. The game begins with each player putting one or more marbles inside the circle (in official tournaments, 13 marbles are placed in the shape of a cross inside the circle). The first player shoots his or her marble (called a "shooter") from outside the circle, attempting to knock one of the marbles inside the circle out. When shooting, at least one knuckle must stay in contact with the ground (see illustration at left for different ways to hold a shooter). If a player is successful at knocking a marble out, that player is granted an additional turn, and can continue shooting as long as he or she knocks a marble out of the circle.

If a shooter remains inside the circle after knocking a marble out, the player's next shot must be made from where the shooter rests. If, after shooting a marble outside the circle, the shooter also comes to rest outside the circle, the player can take a shot from anywhere he or she likes, outside the circle. (See illustration at left for another way to play).

Playing "for keeps" (also called "for fair") means all marbles knocked out of the circle belong to the person who shot them out. Playing "for fun" means the winner is the person who knocks the most marbles outside the circle, but all marbles remain the property of their original owner.

"My mom says she's lost her marbles, but I've never even seen her play."

Marco Polo

It's hard to imagine what that illustrious adventurer of yore would think up this water game, but perhaps the sound of his name being called out, ad infinitum, from one backyard to the next might give him pleasure. It's certainly an interesting variation on "footprints in the sands of time"—something like "echoes in the pools of suburbia."

There are two good things about this game. Your children are getting great exercise without knowing it, and by the very sound of Marco's first and last name, supervising adults can be reasonably sure that everyone in the pool is okay.

Although this game can be played in any body of water, it's much easier on the players if there are distinct, relatively constrained boundaries, such as are found in most swimming pools.

The rules of the game (basically a water version of tag) couldn't be simpler: The person chosen as "It" closes his or her eyes and counts to 50. While "It" is counting, the rest of the players quietly paddle, above or below water, to various parts of the pool, preferably stationing themselves as far as possible from "It."

Once the countdown is complete, "It" begins paddling around, eyes closed, calling out "Marco," to which *all* of the other players must respond, "Polo." "Its" task is to find and tag all the other players. Once tagged, players must remove themselves from the pool. When all of the players have been tagged by "It," the game is over. The next game begins with the first person to have been tagged becoming "It" in the new game.

Marco? Polo. Marco? Polo. Marco? Polo. Where is Polo, anyway? Only a strong, patient swimmer finds out.

Miniature Golf

The creation of a backyard miniature golf course can take the talents and energy of several kids a day or two to produce. Because none of the "improvements" are permanent, no harm is done to lawn or yard. Such a course makes a great centerpiece for a backyard holiday celebration, family barbecue, or any large get-together. And like the "Olympics" on page 69, this is a good multi-generational activity.

The illustration on this page is simply a suggestion, using the type of supplies that might be found around most homes, garages, and basements. Feel free to improvise in any way imaginable.

MINIATURE GOLF

AN IMPROVISED MINIATURE GOLF COURSE CAN BE EASILY MADE FROM OBJECTS FOUND AROUND THE HOUSE OR BASEMENT: A) SHOEBOX, WITH HOLES FRONT AND BACK; B) THREE CROQUET WICKETS IN A ROW; C) A CURVED PIECE OF CLOTHES DRYER VENT HOSE; D) TWO BOARDS, SIDE-BY-SIDE; E) A MOUND OF SAND OR DIRT; F) A BIG PLASTIC POP BOTTLE, TOP AND BOTTOM CUT OUT, LAID AT AN ANGLE; G) AN OLD TIRE, CUT IN HALF AND STAKED TO THE GROUND IN A "LOOP-DE-LOOP" PATTERN; H) THREE BOARDS NAILED TOGETHER TO CREATE A SHOOT, WITH A "FOOT" AT ONE END SO IT SITS AT AN UPWARD ANGLE, AND I), A JUICE CAN, SUBMERGED IN THE SOIL (ITS RIM SHOULD BE JUST AT GROUND LEVEL) TO SERVE AS THE "18TH HOLE." MAKE A HOLE IN ONE ON THIS SHOT, AND WIN EXTRA POINTS OR A SPECIAL PRIZE.

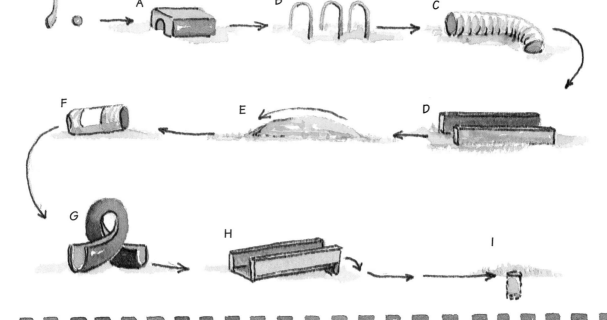

*Staging a backyard
Olympics—be it just for
laughs or to test your strength
and skill—is a sure-fire
recipe for a good time.
Make it a multi-generational
competition and invite
as many neighbors as your
backyard will hold.
Guaranteed good memories!*

Olympics

From Memorial Day to Labor Day, summer offers a number of opportunities for outdoor celebrations. In addition to the already-mentioned summer "bookend" holidays, there's Father's Day, Flag Day, Midsummer's Night (June 21), the Fourth of July, Bastille Day (if you're so inclined), and all manner of picnics, family reunions, and neighborhood get-togethers.

It was in the planning stages for celebrating one of these events that my sister-in-law made the comment, "This year, let's do something besides eat." She had a good point, and I set to work coming up with an activity everyone, young and old, could and (more importantly) *would* want to participate in. That's how the idea for a Backyard Olympics was hatched.

Implicit in any backyard get-together is that it will be informal and, hopefully, fun for everyone involved. Kids can jump and run and yell to their heart's content without much fear of parental interference, and adults, if they are so inclined, can act goofy without risking public humiliation. Why behave when you don't have to, right? With this thought in mind, the first version of the Backyard Olympics involved a high quotient of silliness, reflected in its name, "The Goofball Games."

Over the years we've experimented with another version of the Backyard Olympics—something we call the "Iron Person Competition." This is geared more toward those physical types who like to prove to each other who's the fastest, strongest, or most agile. Both versions of the Backyard Olympics have been deemed a success; the one you choose will probably be based on the participants more than anything else. If it's a mixed-up crowd, feel free to mix and match events from the two versions.

"This was the most fun we had all summer!"

The Goofball Games

The Goofball Games were predicated on the fact that no one wanted to spend a lot of time and money gathering equipment and supplies. All that was required was a morning scavenging for things on hand that might work in a free-for-all competition. Empty plastic pop bottles, old tires, garden hoses, a wheelbarrow, a fishing pole, a plastic baseball bat, and an odd assortment of balls were put into service.

Each of the Goofball Games teams comprised two people—one adult and one child. This left us with two extra adults, who graciously consented to act as official timer/referee and—just in case—medic. The medic may not have been called into action that day, but the referee had her hands full! The adults, it seemed, had a penchant for bending the rules, a fact loudly decried by the kids on opposing teams.

Here's how to begin the games: Mark two sets of identical numbers on small slips of paper and keep them separate. Put the first set into a hat and let the kids pick. Repeat the process for the adults. Match up the numbers and you have your teams. Early on, we decided the event would be more fun without any intra-family teams. After successfully juggling a couple of parent/offspring combinations, we were on our way.

There were seven stations in our original Goofball Games, all of which were set up on the lawn. Each station had preset objectives and rules (sort-of). The stations developed solely from the equipment and supplies we happened to have on hand. Of course you can modify the following any way you want.

Wheelbarrow Road Roll: Hope for a small teammate for this one! A twisting turning course is laid out on the lawn, demarcated by two garden hoses. Put your teammate in the wheelbarrow. Start the stopwatch and stay between the hoses. If you tip over, you have to go back to the start. Fastest time wins.

Wet Pillow Pitch: Water balloons (filled as full as possible) and a pillowcase are all that's needed for this. Standing roughly 20 feet apart, one member of the team pitches the water balloons to his or her teammate, who tries to catch it in the pillowcase—without breaking. This is complicated by the fact that the balloon-thrower must toss the balloons backward, over the shoulder. Three tries; most unbroken water balloons in the pillowcase wins.

Croquet Hole-in-One: Line up three wickets, approximately four feet apart. Plant a stake at the far end. The object is to hit the ball directly through the wickets and hit the stake in one fell stroke. Three tries: most direct hits wins.

Give It Your Best Cast: This one was tough, but we had a few "bobbers-in-one." Fill a wading pool with water. Outfit a casting rod with one of those red-and-white bobbers and a little weight. Standing approximately 20 feet away, try to land the bobber in the wading pool. Five tries (at least!): most bobbers in the pool wins.

Watermelon Wiggle: Grease a watermelon (solid vegetable shortening works best). Put the melon in the wading pool filled with water. Using masking tape, mark an "X" on the lawn about five feet away from the wading pool. Place team members on opposite sides of the pool and instruct them to pick up the melon and place it on the "X." By the way, each team member can use only one hand! Three tries.

Blind-as-a-Bat: Set a plastic "wiffle" ball on a stand. Blindfold the batter and hand him or her a plastic bat. Now, the question is, how far can you hit the ball? Or maybe, can you hit it at all? Five strikes and you're out!

Empty Bottle Bowling: Set up large, empty, plastic pop bottles as you would bowling pins. Position the player approximately 15 to 20 feet away. Then, instead of a ball, roll an empty tire down the "alley." Score as you would traditional bowling.

Just for the record, it took well over two hours for the teams to make it through all seven stations, so you might want to start your party a little earlier than usual.

Wet Pillow Pitch

Empty Bottle Bowling

Croquet Hole-in-One

Wheelbarrow Road Roll

Give It Your Best Cast

Blind-as-a-Bat

Watermelon Wiggle

71

The Iron Person Competition

The first Olympic Games for which there are recorded winners took place in ancient Greece in 776 B.C. The "Games" were confined to one day only, the day of the first full moon after the summer solstice. Interestingly, there was only one event, namely a foot race, approximately 200 yards long. The finishing point was an altar laden with slain animals, fruits, and vegetables. The first person to the altar in 776 B.C. was a man by the name of Coroebus, who, appropriately, was a cook by profession. Upon arriving at the altar, Coroebus was handed a flaming torch to set fire to the offering.

The torch itself had been ignited not by the hand of any mortal, but by directing the sun's reflection off a polished metal bowl, thereby infusing the flames with divinity direct from the sun god. It is not difficult to see the connection between the torch ceremony of today's Olympics and that very early ritual.

By 708 B.C., in addition to the foot race, the Olympic Games had expanded to include leaping, spear throwing, discus throwing, and wrestling competitions. A few years later, boxing and chariot racing were added as well. Individual winners were crowned with a wreath of wild olive branches, given tax exemption for life, and a lifetime seat of honor at the local theater. In addition, the victor's hometown paid to have a statue made of its hero. All things considered, not a bad take.

When planning the Iron Person version of our Backyard Olympics, we took a cue from the ancient games and tried to keep things simple. And while we couldn't offer the winners tax-exempt status for life (a big disappointment!), nor erect statues in their honor, we did create facsimile olive-branch wreaths from sprigs of ivy with which to crown them.

We had six stations in the Iron Person Competition: balance beam, rope climb, bowling ball toss, broad jump, free-form swimming, and, in honor of the original Olympic Games, a 200-yard foot race. Referees required a stop watch (or a watch with a second hand) and a tape measure.

Bowling Ball Toss

Balance Bea[m]

Rope Climb

Broad Jump

Foot Race

Free-form Swimming

Balance beam: This was easily taken care of with a 20-foot-long, two-by-six-inch piece of lumber, which we just happened to have on hand. It was held on edge with a series of small stakes, pounded into the ground on either side. The person with the fastest time from one end to the other, without falling off, was the winner.

Rope climb: This station brought back nightmares from junior high P.E. class for several participants—one look was enough for them to pass. A beefy rope, over 20 feet long, was tied to a sturdy tree limb and, just as in junior high, there were those among us who scrambled up that thing like the proverbial monkey. Fastest time to the top wins.

Bowling ball toss: This was as close as we could come to a shot-put event. One-handed putting only; longest toss wins. No extra points awarded for thrown shoulders.

Broad jump: Just as in the big leagues, but in the absence of a sand lot, make sure the referees are on hand with the tape measure to record the jumps as soon as they are completed. After all, it's hard to preserve a footprint on a lawn. Longest jump wins.

Free-form swimming: The site for our Iron Person Competition was blessed with a swimming pool. The event consisted of five laps of whatever stroke the participant wanted to try. The swimmer with the fastest time wins.

Foot race: Not surprisingly, we didn't have access to a 200-yard-long lawn in our backyard, so we compromised by running the race back and forth between two lines approximately 50 feet apart, twelve times. First one over the line for the twelfth time wins. We saved this event for last, and by the time it was over, even the most competitive players had had their fill for the day.

After the awards ceremony was finished, we had our own "sacrificial offerings" of meat and vegetables, grilled on the barbecue, but offered the delicacies to participants rather than to the gods of yore. It seemed the least we could do after all that exercise. And true to my sister-in-law's request, we had done something that holiday besides eat.

Over-the-Line

Over-the-line is just the thing when a group wants to have the fun of playing baseball, but with a simpler format that takes less time and requires only three persons per team. This is a fast-paced game, great for large outdoor gatherings.

Please note the fact (not mentioned in the rules) that unlike baseball, over-the-line does not involve physically running the bases. A hit puts an imaginary runner on base. Three hits in any one inning constitutes a run; if a teammate hits a home run (after his or her team has hit one or two balls), the home run "clears the bases"—that is, would count as two or three runs, depending on how many "runners" were on base at the time. The following rules were developed by the Old Mission Beach Athletic Club in California:

1) *Players:* Three players per team; substitutes are allowed if a player has not played for any other team. A replaced player may not reenter the game. He or she may, however, play in subsequent games.

2) *At-bat positions:* Bat from home, marked **X**. Teammate pitches from anywhere in front of "the line" or its extensions.

3) *Fielding positions:* Fielders may play anywhere past "the line" or its extensions.

4) *Hits:* A) ball hit into fair territory on the fly without being caught by fielders; B) any ball touched and dropped by fielders; C) fielder crossing "the line" or its extensions when attempting to catch ball (see Rule 12).

5) *Home runs:* Any ball hit past the last fielder in fair territory, on the fly without the fielder touching it. (It only has to go past the fielder, not necessarily over the fielder's head.)

6) *Outs:* A) two foul balls (see Rule 7); B) one strike; C) fly ball caught by a fielder; D) ball hitting "the line" or lines around out area; E) ball touched or dropped by batter or pitcher (see Rule 13-A; foul tips that hit batter and land in foul territory are foul); F) batting out of turn; G) pitcher crossing "the line"

after hit ball (see Rule 12).

7) *Fouls:* A) any ball landing outside "Out" or "Fair" areas on the fly (any ball hitting the foul line, then bouncing back into fair territory, is foul); B) any taken pitch; C) any false pitch or "balk."

8) *Scoring:* A) Three hits in an inning scores one run. Each additional hit in the same inning scores one more run. Home runs "clear the bases." B) Intentional throwing of the bat is a three run penalty (official's decision).

9) *Length of game:* A) Games will be five innings. (Each side gets three outs per inning, like in baseball.) B) If tied at the end of the five, play an additional inning to break the tie. If tied after six, play one more. C) If still tied after seven innings, the team with the most hits is the winner. If a tie exists in hits, play additional innings until the tie is broken, either by hits or by runs. Runs take precedence over hits in this situation. D) If at the end of any inning a team has an eleven or more run lead, the game is over.

10) *Umpiring:* A) Winning team members will be the officials for the next game on the same court. Captain of the winning team will be responsible for keeping track of the game ball. B) Start the game within five minutes after completion of previous game. Any team not ready to play will forfeit; exceptions will be at the discretion of the rules committee. C) Turn in scorecards to official's stand.

11) *Equipment:* A) No gloves are to be used for fielding except in women's division. Taping of hands and fingers is permissible if no padding is used. B) Golf gloves may be used for batting. C) Softball and little league bats only. Furnish your own bats. D) Regulation-size softballs are to be used, and will be furnished by the tournament directors.

12) *Crossing over ("the line"):* A) At no time may players cross from one side of "the line," or its extensions, to the other when catching or attempt-

ing to catch a hit ball. B) You must make a definite stop before crossing the line. If you catch the ball and your momentum carries you into or across the line, it is a penalty (see Rules 4-C and 6-G).

13) *General:* A) A ball caught on the fly by either the batter or pitcher counts as a "no pitch." B) You must have a full team (three players) to start a game. C) No warming up on playing courts. Begin games immediately. D) Decisions of the rules committee are final. © 1975 Old Mission Beach Athletic Club.

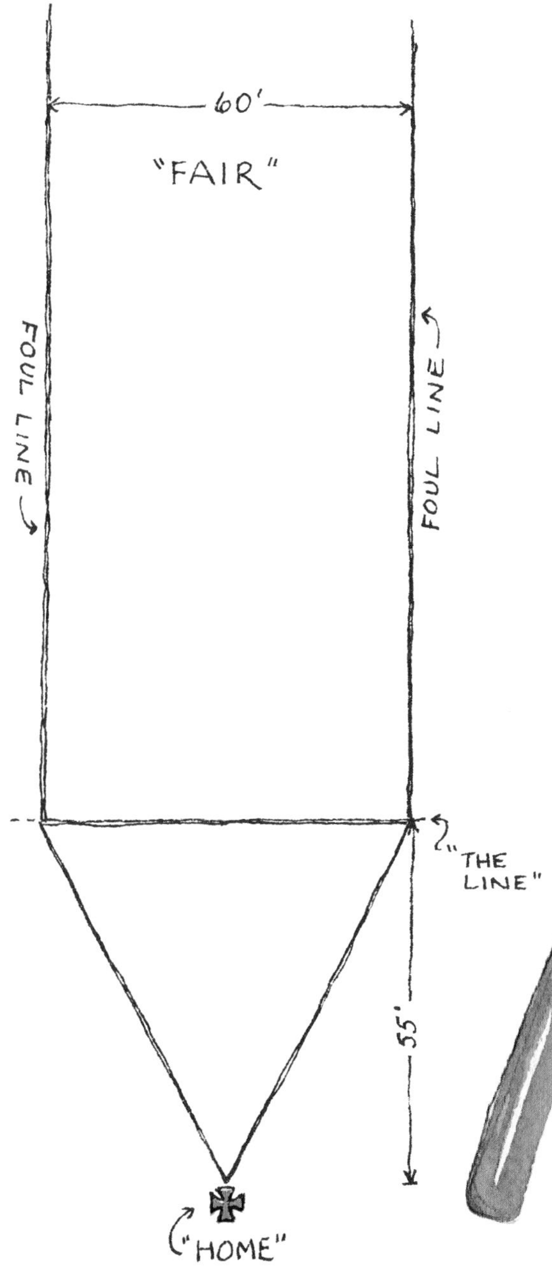

OVER-THE-LINE

PUT SIMPLY, OVER-THE-LINE IS A NON-RUNNING VERSION OF BASEBALL. RUNS ARE SCORED BY HITTING RATHER THAN RUNNING THE BASES.

A TEAM CONSISTS OF THREE PLAYERS. TWO TEAMS PLAY AT A TIME—ONE TEAM IN THE FIELD (ONE PITCHER AND TWO FIELDERS), AND ONE TEAM AT BAT. THE PITCHER MAY STAND ANYWHERE BETWEEN THE "LINE" (SEE DIAGRAM AT LEFT) AND HOME PLATE; FIELDERS STAND BEHIND THE LINE, IN ANY POSITION THEY WANT.

A GAME LASTS FIVE INNINGS. EACH TEAM AT BAT GETS THREE OUTS PER INNING, AS IN BASEBALL. ONE HIT PUTS A PLAYER ON THE IMAGINARY "FIRST BASE"; TWO HITS PUTS PLAYERS ON FIRST AND SECOND. THREE HITS IN AN INNING SCORES ONE RUN. EACH ADDITIONAL HIT IN THIS SAME INNING SCORES ONE MORE RUN. A "HOME RUN" (ANY BALL HIT PAST THE LAST FIELDER IN FAIR TERRITORY, ON THE FLY, WITHOUT THE FIELDER TOUCHING IT) CLEARS THE BASES.

A REGULATION SOFTBALL AND BAT SHOULD BE USED FOR OVER-THE-LINE, BUT GLOVES ARE FORBIDDEN (EXCEPT, ACCORDING TO THE OFFICIAL RULES, IN THE WOMEN'S DIVISION).

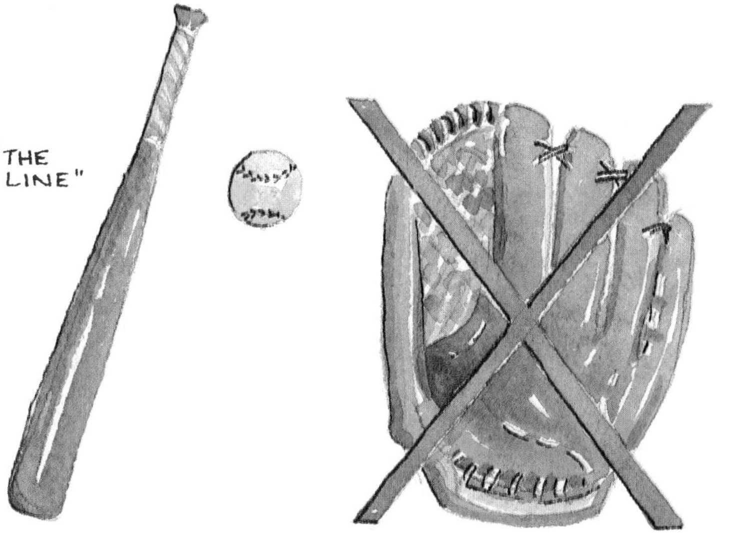

60'

"FAIR"

FOUL LINE

FOUL LINE

"THE LINE"

55'

"HOME"

Piñata

The Mexican piñata has a long history, rich in religious and cultural significance. In Mexico, piñatas—papier-mâché figures, such as donkeys, clowns, or cartoon characters, filled with candy, toys, and other treats—are traditionally associated with Christmas, particularly the posadas celebrations (re-creations of Joseph and Mary's search for lodging on their trek to Bethlehem), held from the 18th to the 24th of December. In more recent times, piñatas have made their appearance at all types of celebrations, from birthday parties to Halloween.

After filling it with whatever treats desired (make sure they're unbreakable), firmly tie a strong cord to the top of the piñata and throw the cord over a beam, tree limb, or, even better, a pulley attached to the ceiling or limb.

The object of the game is to break open the piñata, releasing the bounty inside. To begin, assemble the children in a line. Blindfold the first contestant, spin him (or her) around a few times, hand him a stick or plastic baseball bat and then give him a push in the right direction. To increase the anticipation, give each contestant three swings with the stick or bat. After three tries, the contestant returns to the end of the line.

In the beginning of the game, it's customary for the person hoisting the piñata to keep it bobbing up and down, just out of the bat's reach. As the game progresses, the piñata should be kept within easy hitting range, lest a full-scale riot develop among the kids. Once the piñata disgorges its bounty, the kids will drop to the ground like so many ants on a hill, uproariously grabbing for every treat in sight.

In addition to an adult to pull the piñata up and down, it's a very good idea to have two other adults stationed at the front

Today, piñatas are available in every conceivable style—from cartoon characters to more traditional types. To give the game as much excitement as possible, rig the piñata over a branch or beam, or best of all, on a pulley, to permit easy up-and-down action. A plastic, rather than a wooden bat, packs more than enough wallop to finally break the piñata open, and is a lot safer, as well.

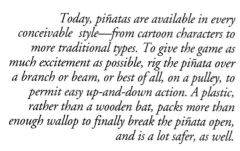

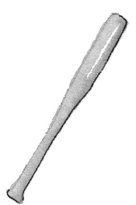

of the line to keep any of the kids from accidentally straying too close to the person who's trying to knock the piñata open. This is especially important when the piñata is about to spill its treasure. At that point, the kids will be in such a frenzy that they're liable to run first and think later.

As simple as this game may be, don't make the mistake of thinking it's too simple or juvenile. The elemental act of breaking open a container full of goodies engages and satisfies all but the most jaded of celebrants.

Predator

Predator would have to be classed as a fairly subtle, "grown-up" game. Even so, kids, depending upon the amount of discretion and guile they possess, will find it engaging—especially if they happen to be the "predator." It may be played indoors or out, but either way, predator is at its most intriguing when played with a large group of people—say at the start of a picnic, a backyard slumber party, or even a camping trip.

Predator is one of the few games where the only person who knows who "it" (the predator) is, is "it" him- or herself. If you're "It," the object of the game is to "kill" everyone at the party without being detected. If you're not "It," the object is to avoid being "killed" by the predator (no easy task) and perhaps to discover who the predator is in the process. Here's how it goes:

The host of the party or event announces to the guests that throughout the evening, or day, or weekend for that matter, the game of predator is going to be played. The host then passes a deck of cards around to the guests (first paring down the pack so the number of cards matches the number of guests exactly, making sure the ace of spades is still in the deck), and asks each person to take one card, look at it without showing anyone else, and give the card back to the host. Whoever receives the ace of spades is the predator.

The host then goes on to explain that the predator is a very deadly character: the predator kills people by merely winking at them! Furthermore, if you are the recipient of a wink from the predator, you must wait at least two or three minutes (much longer, if you want to make the game harder) to announce to the group that you are, in fact, dead. This allows the predator to move to another location to avoid being associated with the death.

As easy as it is for the predator to off someone, it is just as easy to reveal the predator's identity. All that needs to be done is for a third-party observer to catch the predator in the act of winking at one of its prey. If the predator is justly accused, he or she must come clean, and give up the game.

When played by a skillful, discreet predator, one who takes plenty of time between victims, the game can go on, literally, for days.

Indoors, this game usually goes by the name "killer." Outdoors, in a more natural environment, the name "predator" seems far more appropriate.

A wink of the eye is all that it takes to drop players dead in their tracks! A successful game of predator requires a certain amount of subtlety on the part of both the killer and his or her victims. This is a great game for a large outdoor gathering or even a weekend camping trip.

Races

Races are in many ways the most simple and perhaps the most satisfying of games to play in group situations. The races shown here are of the somewhat silly kind, designed to derail those participants for whom winning is everything.

All that's really needed is an open space to run, a way of marking the starting and finish lines, and a referee with a whistle to announce the start and declare the winners.

ABOUT THE ONLY THING YOU CAN DO TO INCREASE YOUR CHANCES OF WINNING A PIGGYBACK RACE IS TO HOPE FOR THE LIGHTEST PIGGY-BACKER AND TELL HIM OR HER TO HOLD ON TIGHT—BUT NOT SO TIGHT THAT YOU END UP IN A "CHOKE HOLD."

WINNING A THREE-LEGGED RACE DEMANDS CLOSE COOPERATION AND A SENSE OF RHYTHM. IF YOU WANT TO MAKE THE RACE MORE DIFFICULT, ONLY USE ONE TIE, AND TIE THE PARTNERS' ANKLES TOGETHER; TO MAKE IT EASIER, USE TWO TIES— ONE TIED AT THE ANKLE AND THE OTHER JUST ABOVE THE KNEE.

THERE ARE TWO SECRETS FOR SUCCESS IN WHEEL-BARROW RACES: 1) INSTRUCT THE WHEELBARROW PARTNER TO KEEP HIS OR HER KNEES AS STRAIGHT AS POSSIBLE, AND 2) HOPE FOR SOMEONE WITH STRONG ARMS. RACERS WHO ARE STRONG ENOUGH WILL ACTUALLY BE ABLE TO "RUN" ON THEIR HANDS.

79

Red Light, Green Light

Red light, green light is a good party game, especially for the younger set. Start by marking two parallel lines on the lawn or pavement (see page 15), at least 25 feet apart.

Choose who will be the first "stoplight" using one of the methods on page 14. Position the stoplight on one of the lines, and all the other players on the opposite line, shoulder-to-shoulder, facing the stoplight.

The stoplight starts the game by announcing a method of locomotion—hopping on two feet, running, skipping, rolling, etc.—and yelling "green light." The contestants then begin hopping, running, skipping, or rolling toward the stoplight until he or she yells "red light." Anyone still in motion after "red light" has been called must return to the starting line. The first person over the stoplight's line becomes the next stoplight.

If only a yellow warning light were included in "red light, green light," it would be a lot easier to play!

Sardines

This is a variation of hide-and-seek that many consider a lot more fun to play. To begin, you should have a minimum of five players—and the more, the merrier. The first person to hide can be determined by drawing straws or by using some other method (see page 14). The hider finds good cover while the rest of the group slowly counts to 100. Upon reaching 100, the group spreads out to hunt for the hider. Instead of announcing the hider's location, like you would in hide-and-seek, the first person to find the hider quietly joins in the hiding. The next person to find the hider joins in as well, until all the players are crammed in the hiding place like sardines in a can. Although it's a nearly impossible task, the hiders should remain as quiet as possible while crammed in their hiding spot. The game is over when the last hunter finds the group. The one who was the first to find the hider becomes the hider in the next game. This game can be played indoors or out, but is especially fun played outdoors, after dark.

Shuffleboard

Shuffleboard began as a type of street game played in England during the Middle Ages. It was known then as "shovel-board." Like most games, it went in and out of fashion (at one time during the 1600s it was relegated back to its humble beginnings and was primarily played in taverns), until someone got the idea to shorten the court (to 28 feet) and install it as a shipboard pastime in the late 1800s. By the early

Sardines need plenty of room to hide in one spot.

81

SHUFFLEBOARD

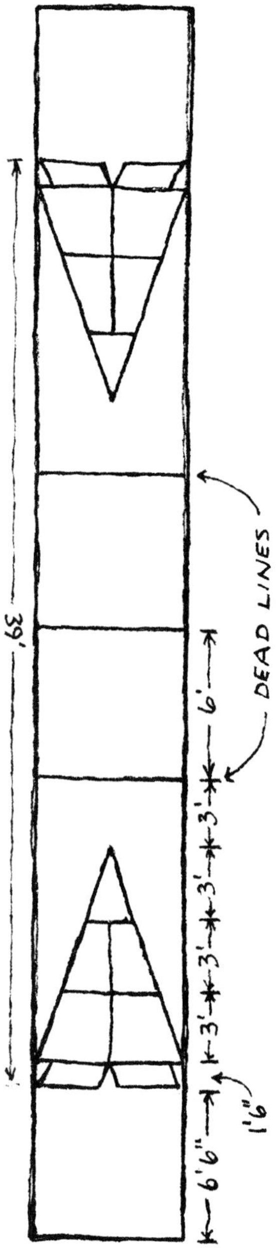

SHUFFLEBOARD HAS GONE IN AND OUT OF FASHION SEVERAL TIMES SINCE THE MIDDLE AGES IN ENGLAND, WHERE IT WAS THEN KNOWN AS "SHOVEL-BOARD." A MUCH SMALLER, TABLETOP VERSION OF THE GAME OF THE SHUFFLEBOARD WAS POPULAR AS AN AFTER-DINNER GAME DURING THE TUDOR ERA.

TODAY'S GAME IS PLAYED ON A COURT THAT'S 6 FEET WIDE AND 52 FEET LONG, AS SHOWN IN THE ILLUSTRATION AT LEFT. THE SURFACE OF THE COURT MUST BE VERY SMOOTH TO ENSURE EASY GLIDING OF THE DISCS.

THE OBJECT OF THE GAME IS TO PUSH YOUR DISC, USING A POLE-LIKE GLIDER, ONTO THE SCORING AREAS OF THE TRIANGLE, WHILE AVOIDING THE "TEN OFF" AREA (DISCS TOUCHING A LINE DO NOT COUNT). THIS FEAT IS HARD ENOUGH, BUT YOU MUST ALSO WATCH FOR YOUR OPPONENT'S ATTEMPTS TO KNOCK YOUR DISCS OFF THE COURT, WHICH *IS* LEGAL IN SHUFFLEBOARD (REMEMBER WHEN IT COME YOUR TURN: "TURN ABOUT IS FAIR PLAY").

SHUFFLEBOARD MAY BE PLAYED WITH TWO OR FOUR PEOPLE; TWO-PERSON GAMES—EACH PERSON PLAYS FOUR DISCS; FOUR-PERSON GAMES (TWO TEAMS OF TWO EACH)—EACH TEAM MEMBER TAKES TURNS PLAYING FOUR DISCS. SCORES ARE TALLIED AFTER EACH SIDE HAS PLAYED THEIR FOUR DISCS. IN DOUBLES PLAY, TEAMMATES PLAY ON OPPOSITE ENDS OF THE COURT, BUT BOTH USE THE SAME COLOR DISCS.

THE AREA WHERE SHUFFLEBOARD PLAY BEGINS IS CALLED THE "HEAD" OF THE COURT, WHILE THE DISCS ARE PUSHED TOWARDS THE "FOOT."

IN OFFICIAL SHUFFLEBOARD TOURNAMENTS A GAME IS PLAYED TO 75 POINTS; A MATCH IS THE BEST TWO OUT OF THREE GAMES.

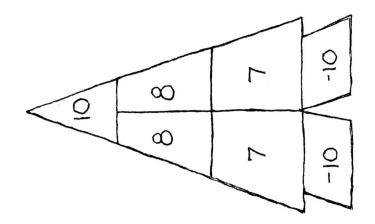

part of this century, a shuffleboard court became a standard feature on all ocean liners, seemingly ensuring the fashionable quality of this game for all time.

The first outdoor shuffleboard courts in this country were built in 1913 in Florida. By 1929, the National Shuffleboard Association had been created. The group did much to popularize the game by standardizing its rules and holding national tournaments, the first of which was held in 1931.

In the United States, a standard shuffleboard court is 52 feet long by 6 feet wide. The most common surface for the court is smooth concrete, but shuffleboard can also be played on wood surfaces, provided they are smooth enough to allow the pucks to slide unimpeded from one end of the court to another. The actual playing area of the shuffleboard court is only 39 feet long.

Shuffleboard can be played by two or four people. Each player or team propels metal pucks down the court using a long pole, which has a special pushing device at the end, into which the puck fits. This polelike object is variously called a cue, a runner, a driver, or a glide.

The object of the game is to score as many points as possible by landing your pucks on the scoring areas (triangular areas painted on the concrete); sections of the scoring area are marked with different scores: 10, 7, 8, and −10. Scores are tallied when each person or team has pushed four pucks.

Play begins at the head of the court, with the pucks being pushed toward the foot of the court. When two teams of doubles play, a member from each team plays at opposite ends of the court.

Pushing a puck across the court so it lands in the scoring area is not all that easy. The game is made even more difficult by the fact that knocking an opponent's puck off the scoring area is permitted. Shuffleboard strategists not only try to keep their opponents from scoring, but try to position their own pucks in such a way as to protect those that have already landed in the scoring area.

An "end" is completed after each side has shot its four pucks. How many ends are played, or what ultimate score constitutes winning, is decided upon before play. Common winning scores are 21, 50, 75, or 100. A match is the best of three games.

The official rules for shuffleboard, as put forth by the National Shuffleboard Association, can be found on page 115.

"Don't tell anyone I told you, but shuffleboard is even more fun when you're wearing Rollerblades."

Simon Says

Any group of three or more people can play this amusing game. The more people who play, however, the more amusing it gets, often bordering on hysterical. The trick is for Simon to feel comfortable issuing rapid-order commands—there's one in every group, isn't there?

To begin play, decide who will be Simon. Line up the other players with some space in between them, facing Simon. The players' task is to do everything "Simon says" to: "Simon says to jump on one foot. Run in place. Scratch your head with both hands. Simon says to make a stupid face," etc., etc. If you had been playing in this game, and had followed only the commands to jump on one foot and to make a stupid face, you'd still be playing. If, however, you ran in place, or scratched your head with two hands, you'd be out, because you never do anything Simon doesn't tell you to do.

Simon says to have fun with this game.

Statue

Here's a classic summertime game to play after dinner, when all you really want is an excuse to roll around on the lawn. No artistic talent is needed: all you need is three or more players. Choose one of the group to be the first sculptor.

The sculptor twirls each player around a couple of times and then instructs him or her to "freeze," usually at the most inopportune moment. When all of the players have become statues, the sculptor walks among them and chooses his or her favorite to become the sculptor in the next game. Everyone knows statues can't move. If any one of them does, it is out of that particular game. It's a good idea to keep a camera handy, as this game can make for some memorable photos.

Sometimes it's the simplest of games that elicit the most laughter. Simon says and statue are two old stand-bys—old, maybe, but not out-of-date. Just try either one at your next backyard gathering and be prepared to be surprised at their durability in the fun department.

Steal the Bacon

When we used to play this game in grammar school, the "bacon" was a blackboard eraser. To my third-grade mind, I was fairly certain the game was called steal the bacon because the eraser, with its alternating black and white stripes, looked a little like a piece of bacon. I'm not so sure now, but back then it gave me something to contemplate while waiting for the referee to call my number.

This irrelevant detail is brought up here for the simple reason that you don't need a blackboard eraser to play this game. A stick, ball, rolled-up newspaper, or anything else that's small and easy to pick up will work just fine. Other than that, you'll need six or more players, divided into equal teams, plus a referee.

Mark two lines on the lawn or pavement, 20 feet or more apart. Arrange the teams on their respective lines, facing each other. Team members should be about five feet apart on the line.

Instruct each team to count off, starting from the left, with an admonition from the referee to "remember your number!" The referee then places the "bacon" in the middle of the space between the two teams and begins the game by calling out a number. The two players with the same number immediately race out to steal the bacon and return home (across the line), before being tagged by the opponent. Each successful trip across the line with the bacon in hand counts one point. If tagged, no point is scored. Either way, the bacon is returned to the middle, and the referee calls a new number. The first team to reach a predetermined number of points wins the game.

STEAL THE BACON

AS NOTED IN THE TEXT AT LEFT, THE "BACON" MAY OR MAY NOT BE A STANDARD BLACKBOARD ERASER. IN FACT, THE "BACON" CAN BE ANYTHING YOU WANT IT TO BE. THE POINT IS TO STEAL THE BACON FROM UNDER YOUR OPPONENT'S NOSE, AND RETURN HOME WITH IT, WITHOUT BEING TAGGED.

THE HARDEST PART OF THIS GAME MAY BE TO REMEMBER YOUR NUMBER AND TO KEEP FROM DAYDREAMING WHILE YOU WAIT FOR IT TO BE CALLED. TAKE MY WORD FOR IT: A LOT OF BACON HAS BEEN LOST WHILE THE POTENTIAL BACON THIEF WAS JUST STANDING AROUND, LOOKING AT THE CLOUDS, WONDERING WHAT WAS FOR LUNCH. SURE ENOUGH ISN'T GOING TO BE BACON, HONEY, IF YOU DON'T WAKE UP AND LOOK LIVELY!

THE "BACON"

Stilts

Everyone should have a pair of stilts at least once in life—if for no other reason than to see what it's like to be a giant, and to feel what it's like to take giant steps. Because stilts are so easy to make and require only a minimum of materials, tools, and carpentry skills, they represent a good building project for kids.

For a while there, way back when, it seemed like everyone in my neighborhood had a pair of stilts. As these things went, the first person to have a pair would be responsible for showing everyone else how to make them. I recall one memorable stilt parade, staged to announce a backyard circus we were holding at a friend's house. Viewed from afar, we must have looked like a swarm of praying mantises coming down the street.

Surprisingly easy to learn to use, stilts can be built from the simplest of material ...

While it's fun to parade around on your stilts, it's also possible to use them for a variety of games. Just make sure all your friends have stilts, too. You can stage different types of stilt races or stilt obstacle courses. All things considered, stilts are probably less dangerous than skateboards or rollerblades, but to avoid injury, any races are best run as timed, solo events. There's just too great a chance for someone getting hurt in a field of stilts to take the risk.

In Java they have a special stilt race. Adults string a cord between two trees, just about at mouth height (measured when the players are on their stilts) and hang pieces of cake and cookies from the cord. The object is to race up to the cord and then eat the cookie or cake without using your hands. Try that at your next birthday party!

... if there's no lumber available, try making a pair from a couple of tomato juice cans and some twine, as shown above.

Tag

There are countless variations on the "tag, you're it!" theme, all of them revolving around one "It," who tries to tag the others. Tag games have been played forever, on virtually every continent. Long ago, tag was a convenient way of teaching children some of the more important aspects of hunting—the need to be agile and swift of foot—while having fun in the process. The notion of a home base, often the trunk of a large tree, as a place of safety also dates back to antiquity when trees were often thought of as possessing a benign spirit.

The rules for the various tag games are virtually the same. The person chosen as "It" (see page 14) tries to tag the other players, rendering them "out." The first person "It" tags is usually "It" in the next game. The game can be over in one of three ways: 1) as soon "It" tags his or her first victim; 2) when "It" has tagged all the players, or 3) when all the players have safely tagged "home," in which case "It" is "It" again for the next game.

In some variations of tag, a player can touch another player, previously tagged by "It" and therefore out of the game, magically restoring them to the game. In other variations, if just one person makes it to home base, all the "out" players are set fee. And in case you wondering, this is the origin of that famous line: "Olly, olly, oxen free." Get it? It really means "all the, all the outs are free."

Illustrated at right are just a few of the tag variations with timeless appeal.

THIS IS A SIMPLE BUT FUN VERSION OF TAG. PICK A SUNNY DAY TO PLAY, OR THERE WON'T BE ANY SHADOWS FOR "IT" TO STEP ON! DECIDE ON A HOME BASE. WITH A PREDETERMINED SIGNAL, THE GAME BEGINS WITH ALL THE PLAYERS STANDING CLOSE TOGETHER. IF "IT" STEPS ON YOUR SHADOW BEFORE YOU REACH HOME, YOU'RE OUT.

START A GAME OF ANKLE TAG BY CHOOSING WHO WILL BE "IT." OTHER PLAYERS THEN SCATTER TO THE WIND WHILE "IT" TRIES TO TAG THEM. INSTEAD OF A HOME BASE, PLAYERS ARE SAFE FROM BEING TAGGED AS LONG AS THEY ARE HOLDING ONE OF THEIR ANKLES.

WAIT UNTIL DARK. DECIDE ON A HOME BASE, CHOOSE WHO WILL BE "IT," AND HAND HIM OR HER A FLASHLIGHT. "IT" HIDES HIS OR HER EYES, COUNTS TO 100, AND SHOUTS "READY OR NOT, HERE I COME!" "IT" GETS PLAYERS OUT BY CATCHING THEM IN THE BEAM OF THE FLASHLIGHT AND CALLING OUT THEIR NAME BEFORE THEY CAN REACH HOME BASE.

IN THIS VERSION OF TAG, IF "IT" TAGS YOU BEFORE YOU REACH HOME, YOU MUST FREEZE AND STAY FROZEN UNTIL ANOTHER PLAYER TOUCHES YOU AND THAWS YOU OUT. THE GAME IS OVER WHEN EVERYONE IS FROZEN STIFF, OR HOME FREE —ONE OR THE OTHER!

ALAN MAY

Tetherball

Mary Ann Turconi was one of the smallest (and cutest) girls in my third grade class. She was also the most vicious tetherball player in the school. Witnessing Mary Ann in a blur of action as she took down another challenger, I first got the notion that life was going to be a lot more interesting and challenging than I had previously thought.

A tetherball is unique in the world of balls: it's the only ball with a built-in loop for attaching it to a rope. The free end of the 7-foot rope is then attached to the top of a 9-foot metal pole. The pole, in turn, is firmly positioned on some type of hard surface, such as concrete or asphalt. Mark a circle, 20-feet in diameter, on the pavement, with the pole at the center. Next, mark lines on the circle as shown in the illustration below.

To begin a game of tetherball, two opponents stand inside their respective playing zones, more or less opposite one another. Choose the person who will serve first (see page 14). The first person to serve has his or her choice of hitting to the right or the left. This done, the opponent tries to hit the ball back in the opposite direction. Each player must stay within his or her own playing zone. The object of the game, for anyone who may have forgotten, is to see who can wind the ball, in their chosen direction, completely around the pole.

Mary Ann's secret, if I recall it correctly, had to do with hitting the ball very hard and at such an angle that when it reached the opponent, most of the time it was above the opponent's head. What a neat trick!

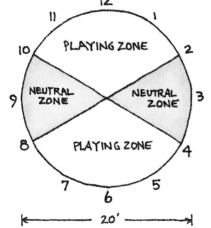

TETHERBALL

A TETHERBALL COURT IS A CIRCLE, 20-FEET IN DIAMETER, DIVIDED INTO TWO PLAYING ZONES AND TWO NEUTRAL ZONES. BY A CLOCK DIAL, THESE DESIGNATIONS WOULD BE MARKED BY LINES BETWEEN 2 AND 8 O'CLOCK AND BETWEEN 4 AND 10 O'CLOCK, AS SHOWN ABOVE.

TO PLAY TETHERBALL, ONE PLAYER STANDS IN EACH COURT. THE SERVER STARTS THE GAME BY TOSSING THE BALL INTO THE AIR AND STRIKING IT IN ANY DIRECTION, THE OPPONENT MAY NOT STRIKE THE BALL UNTIL IT PASSES ON ITS SECOND SWING AROUND THE POLE. AS THE BALL TRAVELS, EACH PLAYER TRIES TO HIT IT IN AN EFFORT TO WIND THE ROPE COMPLETELY AROUND THE POLE. THE PLAYER WHO FIRST WINDS THE ROPE COMPLETELY AROUND THE POLE IN THE DIRECTION OF HIS OR HER PLAY, WINS THE GAME. DURING THE GAME EACH PLAYER MUST REMAIN IN HIS OR HER OWN PLAYING ZONE. FOULS: 1) HITTING THE BALL WITH ANY PART OF THE BODY OTHER THAN THE HANDS OR FOREARMS; 2) STOPPING CONTINUOUS PLAY BY HOLDING OR CATCHING THE BALL; 3) TOUCHING THE POLE WITH ANY PART OF THE BODY; 4) INTERFERING WITH THE PROGRESS OF THE GAME BY HITTING THE ROPE; 5) PLAYING THE BALL WHILE STANDING OUTSIDE THE PLAYING ZONE. PENALTIES: A PLAYER WHO COMMITS ANY FOUL FORFEITS THE GAME TO THE OPPONENT. PLAY STOPS IMMEDIATELY AFTER A FOUL HAS BEEN COMMITTED. SCORING: THE GAME IS WON BY THE PLAYER WHO FIRST WINDS THE ROPE COMPLETELY AROUND THE POLE, OR BY FORFEIT BECAUSE OF A FOUL COMMITTED BY HIS OR HER OPPONENT. A SET CONSISTS OF FOUR GAMES WON OUT OF SEVEN. AFTER THE FIRST GAME, THE WINNER SERVES FIRST.

Treasure Hunt

A treasure hunt can provide one of the richest memories of childhood, or it can be a flash-in-the-pan event that's over practically before it's begun—it all depends on the amount of preparation that has gone into it.

The key to success is in the clues. If you're in charge of coming up with the clues for a treasure hunt, temporarily throw off those constraining, boring old shackles of adulthood, and approach the activity with all the impracticality and wild abandon of a 10-year-old. The fact is, if in the writing of the clues the organizer becomes excited and engaged, the participants undoubtedly will, too.

Above all, don't make the clues too easy! When a group of kids gets together to try and figure something—*anything*—out, they show remarkable intuition and intelligence. Make it tough on them. They can always ask for additional clues, if necessary—a far better situation than having them run easily from one clue to the next, arriving at the "treasure" without enough consternation and anticipatory anxiety. This is a situation where getting there is almost all of the fun.

Give yourself a few days to think about the site, work on the clues, and bury the treasure. Make sure none of the participants see you leaving the clues (never put them in plain sight) or hiding the treasure. Consider writing the first clue as part of a letter from a fictitious person. Send the letter to yourself (this will give it an air of authenticity), and start the game by telling the players that you "received the strangest letter the other day . . ." The letter can both describe how the former owners of the land or house buried a treasure on the property, and supply the first clue. You'd be surprised how effective this ploy can be. The crew will be off and running faster than you can say "Long John Silver."

Party-supply and dime stores usually have a ready supply of plastic jewels, coins, paper money, and other assorted bijoux, just right for running one's hands through, exclaiming "we're rich, we're rich!" And if you're looking for something to use as the treasure chest, cigar boxes (which most smoke shops will give away for free) work great.

As an added bonus, consider putting one last clue in the treasure chest—something about meeting at the ice cream shop for a free cone.

Although real treasure chests are few and far between, a wooden cigar box is an acceptable substitute. Most smoke shops give them away for free.

Tug-of-War

Tug-of-war is probably one of the oldest and most universal of all games, and some form of modern-day tug of war continues to be played in virtually every country. Old beliefs die hard, and even today, the results of some tug-of-wars are said to determine everything from the severity of the upcoming winter, to the size of the next harvest, to whether or not rain will fall.

A desire to predict some aspect of the future is not a necessity to stage a tug-of-war; they're great fun as a simple test of strength and skill and almost a sure bet for plenty of laughter, from both contestants and onlookers. Official games are played with two teams of eight persons each; in reality, they can be staged with any size group (just make sure your rope is long enough). The most interesting (and longest running) games are those where the two sides are, overall, fairly evenly matched in terms of size, strength, and weight.

To play a game of tug-of-war, find a sturdy rope, at least 60 feet in length (for two teams of eight) and some black electrician's tape. Locate the center of the rope and mark it with a band of the tape. Choose an area large enough to accommodate the game and attendant fallout. Lay the rope on

There's nothing quite like a tug-of-war as the centerpiece of a big outdoor gathering. As in the game of capture the flag, tug-of-war plays to the most fundamental feelings of competition: us against you. If there's someone in the group who doesn't feel up to the challenge, hand them a video camera to record the event for future entertainment!

the ground, in a straight line. Make a mark on the ground directly under the center mark on the rope.

Each team elects a captain (which should not be the largest or heaviest person; save that person to use as the "anchor"). Once chosen, each captain arranges his or her team along the rope, three to five feet apart, with an empty space for him- or herself at the head of the line, approximately 10 feet from the center marker on the rope. Position the "anchor" as the last person in line (don't forget to leave the anchor with some rope to play out, should that become a necessity). Once the teams are in position along the rope, the captains take their respective positions at the head of the lines and instruct their teams to stand by the ready. The referee makes sure the center mark of the rope is directly over the mark on the ground and at the sound of the bell (or whatever), the tug—or the war—begins.

The first team to pull the captain of the opposing side over the mark on the ground is declared the winner.

Just imagine how much fun this game is when the center mark is in the middle of a mud hole: that's how tug-of-war is played some places. How wild and woolly you make this game is up to you.

Two Square

Two square, an interesting, outdoor variation of table tennis, can be played on any paved surface. To play you'll need two people, a piece of chalk to mark the court, and a small rubber ball. If you really want to make things interesting, use a "super" ball—the kind that bounces much higher than normal.

Begin by marking two squares (which share the center line) on the pavement, approximately four feet square. Choose who will be the first to serve the ball (see page 14). Both the server and the receiver stand outside the back line of the square during the serve, but may move into the square subsequently.

Instead of paddles or rackets, players use the palms of their hands to serve and hit the ball. One bounce is allowed on each side.

If the receiver fails to return the ball, or returns it out of bounds, the server wins one point; the server is the only one who can score a point. If the server delivers the serve out of bounds or loses the ensuing rally, the serve rotates to the other player. The winner of a point always controls the serve.

Play to a preset score—usually 21. The game must be won by two points, however, so it is possible to play to a higher score.

TWO SQUARE

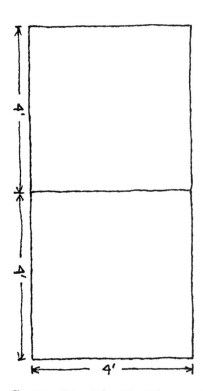

TWO SQUARE IS BASICALLY A VARIATION ON THE GAME OF PING-PONG—IT'S JUST PLAYED ON THE PAVEMENT INSTEAD OF A PING-PONG TABLE, AND YOU USE YOUR HANDS INSTEAD OF A PADDLE. ALTHOUGH A RUBBER PLAYGROUND BALL IS USUALLY USED FOR TWO SQUARE, ANY BALL WILL DO, INCLUDING A TENNIS BALL, OR ONE OF THE SUPER BOUNCY SUPER BALLS.

MARK THE COURT ON ANY FAIRLY SMOOTH PAVE-MENT, AS SHOWN IN THE ILLUSTRATION AT LEFT, WITH A PIECE OF CHALK. START THE GAME BY CHOOSING WHO WILL GO FIRST. THE SERVE IS DONE FROM OUTSIDE THE SQUARE, BUT THE BALL MUST ALWAYS LAND INSIDE THE SQUARE, AND MAY ONLY BOUNCE ONCE BEFORE RETURNING IT TO THE OTHER SIDE.

A RUBBER PLAYGROUND BALL
IS THE NORMAL BALL OF
CHOICE FOR TWO SQUARE,
BUT ONE OF THOSE
LITTLE "SUPER BALLS"
WILL LIVEN UP THE GAME!

Volleyball

The American version of volleyball is an adaptation of a late 19th century German game known as *Faustball*. The Germans had, in turn, imported the game from Italy, where it had been played since the Middle Ages.

In 1895, the physical education director of the Young Men's Christian Association of Holyoke, Massachusetts, William G. Morgan, revised the German game and renamed it mintonette. Morgan originally conceived of mintonette as an indoor game, designed for older members of society who found other outdoor sports too strenuous—somewhat ironic, when today's beachfront game is considered.

Morgan's game of mintonette differed from *Faustball* in two important ways: first, the ball was not permitted to hit the floor (in *Faustball* the ball could bounce twice before being returned), and second, instead of a rope stretched across the middle of the court, mintonette called for the use of a net. Morgan's changes have endured, but his name for the game has not. Noting the volleying nature of the game, Dr. Alfred Halstead, a colleague of Morgan's, suggested the name "volleyball," and so it has been ever since.

Equipment needed for volleyball includes only the volleyball itself and a 32-foot-long, 39-inch-wide net, with poles and anchors for stretching tightly across the court. The net is placed across the middle of a court, approximately 30 by 60 feet (an official court is 29' 6" by 59'), with the top of the net measuring seven feet, eleven inches above the ground.

Volleyball games can be played on almost any surface, but sand or grass is the best for cushioning falls—not uncommon in today's spirited game. Tournament games are played with six players to a side.

Do you know all about dinking, roll shots, cobras, and camel toes? If not, you might want to check page 122, in the official outdoor volleyball rules, to see what your game has been missing.

VOLLEYBALL

VOLLEYBALL HAS ENJOYED A HUGE INCREASE IN POPULARITY IN RECENT YEARS, OWING IN LARGE PART TO THE GAME BEING PLAYED OUTDOORS, PARTICULARLY AT THE BEACH. IF THERE ISN'T A BEACH AROUND THE CORNER FROM WHERE YOU LIVE, IT'S STILL POSSIBLE TO EXPERIENCE THE ACTION AND EXCITEMENT OF THE GAME—SAY, ON THE LAWN, IN YOUR BACKYARD. IT MAY NOT BE QUITE AS VISUALLY STIMULATING, BUT THE GRASS IS COOLER THAN SAND AND THE BATH-ROOMS ARE A LOT CLOSER ...

AN OFFICIAL VOLLEYBALL COURT MEASURES 59 FEET LONG BY 29 FEET, 6 INCHES WIDE. THE NET, WHICH SHOULD MEASURE AT LEAST 32 FEET IN LENGTH AND 39 INCHES IN WIDTH, IS PLACED IN THE MIDDLE OF THE COURT. THE HEIGHT OF THE TOP OF THE NET, AT THE CENTER OF THE COURT, SHOULD MEASURE 7 FEET, 11 INCHES FROM THE GROUND FOR MEN'S TOURNAMENT PLAY, AND 7 FEET, 4 INCHES FOR WOMEN'S TOURNAMENTS. THE OFFICIAL RULE BOOK DOESN'T ADDRESS THE HEIGHT OF THE NET FOR CO-ED GAMES; PERHAPS YOU SHOULD SPLIT THE DIFFERENCE AND ADJUST THE NET TO 7 FEET, 7½ INCHES?

INTERESTINGLY, THE OFFICIAL RULE BOOK *DOES* DEVOTE A GREAT DEAL OF SPACE TO THE SUBJECT OF MISCONDUCT AND THE PENALTIES INCURRED FOR "MISCONDUCTING." LACKING AN OFFICIAL REFEREE IN YOUR BACKYARD, ALL OF THIS CAN BE COMPLETELY IGNORED AND YOU CAN MISCONDUCT TO YOUR HEART'S CONTENT. WHY BEHAVE WHEN YOU DON'T HAVE TO?

59'

29' 6"

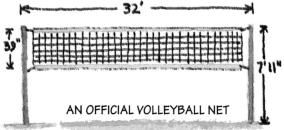

32'

39"

7' 11"

AN OFFICIAL VOLLEYBALL NET

Only the serving team can score a point. The player at right back serves the ball while standing behind the baseline. The served ball must clear the top of the net and stay within the boundaries of the opposite side of the court. If the opposing side does not successfully return the ball over the net, in a maximum number of three hits, the serving side scores a point. If the server fails to serve the ball successfully, play goes to the opposite side, although no point is scored by the opposing team.

Never let the ball touch the ground inside your own court; doing so results in a point scored or a side-out for the opposing team. The first team to score 15 points is declared the winner. In the case of a 14-to-14 tie, the winner will be the first team to lead by two points.

There are three styles of serving the ball in volleyball: underhand, overhand, and sidearm. While the underhand serve is the most popular and easiest to control, the overhand serve is considerably faster and harder to return, as is the sidearm serve, although to a lesser extent. It's best to start with the underhand serve, especially in competitive play, practicing the overhand or sidearm serve on your own. Once perfected, these two serves can be deadly to the opposition.

Generally speaking, a back-line player (known as a "stopper") receives the serve, hitting to a forward teammate (known as the "set-up" or "booster") who, in turn, sets up a high shot to be slammed into the opposing court by a neighboring front-line player, known as the "spiker." This slam shot requires leaping into the air and hitting the ball sharply with the heel of the palm, and is often unreturnable by the opposing team.

With the exception of plain-old fumbles by the opposition, most points in volleyball are won by the offensive tactics of the spiker—that player in the front row who hammers the ball into the opposing court. To be most effective, the spiker should aim the ball into an unprotected "hole" on the opposing side. If the spiker has been properly set up by the booster—with a lofty ball 10 to 15 feet high, about a foot or so from the net—he or she should jump into the air as high as possible and slam the ball at a downward angle with great force. Varying this procedure also has its rewards, however. Many points have been won by a spiker who only pretends that the ball is about to be slammed, with great war-cries and much grimacing, and then merely taps the ball barely over the net. Imagine their surprise!

While spiked balls are difficult to return, they can be blocked by one or two receivers who jump up on the other side of the net, arms outstretched, palms open and together. This move not only takes guts, but timing—especially if two teammates try to do it in unison. The object, of course, is to simply meet the spiked ball "head-on" with your open palms, deflecting the speeding ball directly back over the net. Good luck.

The official rules for outdoor volleyball, as put forth by the United States Volleyball Association, can be found on page 118.

Junior Volleyball

The United States Volleyball Association has approved a variation of volleyball for junior players. Interestingly, it contains many of the rules from Mr. Morgan's original game of mintonette, from way back there in 1895.

For junior volleyball, the net should be lowered to seven feet, and the court reduced to 40-by-20 feet. The server has two tries to get the ball over the net, teammate-assisted, if necessary. If desired, the server may also stand in the center of the back court for serving. After a successful serve, the ball can be hit as many times as is necessary to return it over the net. Individuals may hit the ball more than once in succession.

Winning is important in some situations, but when it's all said and done (with apologies to John Lennon), "the fun you take is equal to the fun you make." When it comes to having fun, there's simply no better place than your own backyard. Here's to all you funsters: Have a ball!

(P.S. In case you were wondering, that's my mom in the picture, attempting a handstand in Florida, c. 1945. Isn't it a good thing to know that somewhere, at some point, your mom could do a handstand?)

EPILOGUE—SPRING, 1993

There was a time, not that long ago, when entire towns and villages turned out to see one sort of game or another. Toothless eight-month-olds and equally toothless eighty-year-olds stood on the sidelines to witness everyone in between participate in every sort of contest, from barrel rolling, to foot races, to log rolls, and even competitions where a giant ball stayed in play (without ever touching the ground) for an entire day.

I know this wasn't all that long ago because there are photographs to prove it took place, and photography itself has not been around for all that long. Some of these fragile, sepia-toned memorials to fun gone by are, happily, contained in albums close at hand. I may be guilty of romanticizing an earlier time, but my heart tells me these are activities worth romanticizing.

The gulf between childhood and adulthood is a wide and mysterious one—especially to a child. That separation is narrowed somewhat when adults, either by choice or by custom, include children in their work and, perhaps more importantly, in their play.

The desire to play, spiced with good-natured competition, is both universal and timeless. It does not belong to any one culture, any particular era, and certainly not to any one age group. The backyard is a wonderfully level playing field, where everyone is invited, anyone can join in, and where in addition to the joy of the moment, there is the possibility of making memories that will last a lifetime, or more.

A.C.S.
Spring, 1993

"Just because it's dark, doesn't mean we have to stop playing, you know …"

APPENDIX
OFFICIAL RULES

OFFICIAL RULES

Badminton

The following rules of play are excerpted from the "Official Rules of Play," as adopted by the United States Badminton Association:

Players. "Player" applies to all those taking part in a match. The game shall be played, in the case of doubles, by two players a side, or in the case of singles, by one player a side. The side having the right to serve shall be called the serving side, and the opposing side shall be called the receiving side.

Toss. Before commencing play, the opposing sides shall toss and the side winning the toss shall exercise the choice of a) to serve or receive first or b) to start play at one end of the court or the other. The side losing the toss shall then exercise the remaining choice.

Scoring. The opposing sides shall play the best of three games unless otherwise arranged. Only the serving side can add a point to its score. In doubles and men's singles, a game is won by the first side to score fifteen points (except when the game has been "set"). In women's singles, a game is won by the first side to score 11 points (except when the game has been "set").

Setting the Game. If the score becomes 13 all or 14 all (9 all or 10 all in women's singles), the side that first scored 13 or 14 (9 or 10) shall have the choice of "setting" or "not setting" the game. The choice can only be made when the score is first reached and must be made before the next service is delivered.

The relevant side is given the opportunity to set at 14 all (10 all in women's singles) despite any previous decision not to set by that side or the opposing side at 13 all (9 all in women's singles). If the game has been set, the score is called "Love All" and the side first scoring the set number of points wins the game: a) 13 all setting to 5 points, b) 14 all setting to 3 points, c) 9 all setting to 3 points, or d) 10 all setting to 2 points. The side winning a game serves first in the next game.

Change of Ends. Players shall change ends: a) at the end of the first game, b) prior to the beginning of the third game (if any); and c) in the third game, or in a one-game match, when the leading score reaches 6 in a game of 11 points, 8 in a game of 15 points, or 11 in a game of 21 points.

When players omit to change ends as indicated above, they shall do so when the mistake is discovered and the existing score shall stand.

Service. In a correct service, neither side shall cause undue delay to the delivery of the service. The server and receiver shall stand within diagonally opposite service courts without touching the boundary lines of these service courts; some part of both feet of the server and receiver must remain in contact with the surface of the court in a stationary position until the service is delivered.

The server's racket shall initially hit the base of the shuttle while the whole of the shuttle is below the server's waist. The shaft of the server's racket at the instant of hitting the shuttle shall be pointing in a downward direction to such an extent that the whole of the head of the racket is discernible below the whole of the server's hand holding the racket.

The movement of the server's racket must continue forward after the start of the service until the service is delivered. The flight of the shuttle shall be upward from the server's racket to pass over the net, so that, if not intercepted, it falls in the receiver's service court.

Once the players have taken their positions, the first forward movement of the server's racket is the start of the service. The server shall not serve before the receiver is ready, but the receiver shall be considered to have been ready if a return of the service is attempted. The service is delivered when, once started, the shuttle is hit by the server's racket or the shuttle lands on the floor. In doubles, the partners may take up any positions that do not unsight the opposing server or receiver.

Singles. The players shall serve from, and receive in, their respective right service courts when the server has not scored or has scored an even number of points in that game. The players shall serve from, and receive in, their respective left service courts when the server has scored an odd number of points in that game. If a game is set, the total points scored by the server in that game shall be used to apply.

The shuttle is hit alternately by the server and the receiver until a "fault" is made or the shuttle ceases to be in play. If the receiver makes a "fault" or the shuttle ceases to be in play because it touches the surface of the court inside the receiver's court, the server scores a point. The server then serves again from the alternate service court.

If the server makes a "fault" or the shuttle ceases to be in play because it touches the surface of the court inside the server's court, the server loses the right to continue serving, and the receiver then becomes the server, with no point scored by either player.

Doubles. At the start of a game, and each time a side gains the right to serve, the service shall be delivered from the right service court. Only the receiver shall return the service: should the shuttle touch or be hit by the receiver's partner, the serving side scores a point.

After the service is returned, the shuttle is hit by either player of the serving side and then by either player of the receiving side, and so on, until the shuttle ceases to be in play. After the service is returned, a player may hit the shuttle from any position on that player's side of the net.

If the serving side makes a "fault" or the shuttle ceases to be in play because it touches the surface of the court inside the serving side's court, the server loses the right to continue serving, with no point scored by either side. The player who serves at the start of any game shall serve from, or receive in, the right service court when that player's side has not scored or has scored an even number of points in that game, and the left service court otherwise.

The player who receives at the start of any game shall receive in, or serve from, the right service court when that player's side has not scored or has scored an even number of points in that game, and the left service court otherwise. The reverse pattern applies to partners. If a game is set, the total points scored by a side in that game shall be used to apply the above.

Service in any turn of serving shall be delivered from alternate service courts, except as provided below. The right to serve passes consecutively from the initial server in any game to the initial receiver in that game, and then consecutively from that player to that player's partner and then to one of the opponents and then the opponent's partner, and so on.

No player shall serve out of turn, receive out of turn, or receive two consecutive services in the same game, except as provided below. Either player of the winning side may serve first in the next game, and either player of the losing side may receive.

Service Court Errors. A service court error has been made when a player: a) has served out of turn; b) has served from the wrong service court; or c) standing in the wrong service court, was prepared to receive the service and it has been delivered.

When a service court error has been made, then: a) if the error is discovered before the next service is delivered, it is a "let," unless only one side was at fault and lost the rally, in which case the error shall not be corrected; b) if the error is not discovered before the next service is delivered, the error shall not be corrected; c) if there is a "let" because of a service court error, the rally is replayed with the error corrected. If a service court error is not to be corrected, play in that game shall proceed without changing the players' new service courts (nor, when relevant, the new order of serving).

Faults. It is a fault: a) if a service is not corrected (see above); b) if the server, in attempting to serve, misses the shuttle; c) if after passing over the net on service, the shuttle is caught in or on the net; d) if in play, the shuttle lands outside the boundaries of the court; passes through or under the net; fails to pass the net; touches the roof, ceiling, or side walls; touches the person or dress of a player; or touches any other object or person outside the immediate surroundings of the court; and e) if, when in play, the initial point of contact with the shuttle is not on the striker's side of the net. (The striker may, however, follow the shuttle over the net with the racket in the course of a stroke.)

It is also a fault if, when the shuttle is in play, a player: a) touches the net or its supports with racket, person, or dress; b) invades an opponent's court with racket or person in any degree except as permitted above; c) prevents an opponent from making a legal stroke where the shuttle is followed over the net; d) deliberately distracts an opponent by any action such as shouting or making gestures.

It is a fault if, in play, the shuttle: a) is caught and held on the racket and slung during the execution of a stroke; b) is hit twice in succession by the same player with two strokes (a double hit by one player with one stroke is not a fault); c) is hit by a player and the player's partner successively; or d) touches a player's racket and continues toward the back of that player's court.

It is also a fault if a player is guilty of flagrant, repeated, or persistent offenses.

Lets. "Let" is called by the umpire, or by a player (if there is no umpire) to halt play. A "let" may be given for any unforeseen or accidental occurrence. If a shuttle, after passing over the net, is caught in or on the net, it is a "let," except during service. If during service, the receiver and server are both faulted at the same time, it shall be a "let."

If the server serves before the receiver is ready, it shall be a "let." If during play, the shuttle disintegrates and the base completely separates from the rest of the shuttle, it shall be a "let." If a line judge is unsighted and the umpire is unable to make a decision, it shall be a "let."

When a "let" occurs, the play since the last service shall not count, and the player who serves shall serve again, except as stated above under *Service Court Errors.*

Shuttle Not in Play. A shuttle is not in play when: a) it strikes the net and remains attached there or suspended on top; b) it strikes the net or post and starts to fall toward the surface of the court on the striker's side of the net; c) it hits the surface of the court; or d) a "fault" or "let" has occurred.

Bocce

The following guidelines for play are excerpted from *Bocce*, printed in Italy and distributed by Sportcraft, a U.S. manufacturer of sporting equipment.

The Game. Bocce is played with eight large balls and one smaller target or object ball called the pallino or jack. There are four balls to a side, or team, and they are made in two colors to distinguish the balls of one team from those of the other team. A coin toss determines which team has the pallino and which color balls that team selects.

The pallino is thrown out by a member of the team having won the coin toss to start the game. The same player throwing the pallino must deliver the first bocce ball.

The opposing team will then deliver their bocce balls until the point is taken or they have exhausted their four balls. This "nearest" ball rule governs the sequence of thrown balls. The side whose bocce is closest to the pallino is called the "in" ball and the opposing side the "out" ball. Whenever a team gets "in" it steps aside and allows the "out" team to bowl.

A team has the option of rolling, throwing, bouncing, banking, etc., its ball down the court, provided it does not go out of bounds or the player does not violate the foul markers. A player also has the option of "spocking" or hitting out any ball in play in trying to

obtain a point, or decreasing the opposing team's points.

At the end of each frame (when both teams have exhausted four balls each), a designated official under the scrutiny of the captain or designee of each team, will determine the points scored. Scoring points are all those balls of one team closer to the pallino than the closest ball of the opposing team, which can be determined by viewing or by mechanical measurement.

In the event that the two balls closest to the pallino belong to opposing teams and are tied, no points will be awarded, and the pallino returns to the team that delivered it. Only balls that are distinguishably closer to the pallino than any opponent's balls may be awarded points.

Scoring. The frames shall be scored as follows: four-man teams (one ball per player), 16 points; three-man teams (one ball per player), 16 points; two-man teams (two balls per player), 16 points; one-man teams (four balls per player), 11 points.

Definition of Terms and Faults. The rules for bocce are quite straightforward, but the few definitions and list of fouls that follow may come in handy. For information on court size and markings, please see page 29.

Live Ball—Any ball in play or waiting to be thrown is considered a live ball.

Dead Ball—Any ball that has been disqualified. A ball may be disqualified if: a) it is the result of a penalty; b) it has gone out of the court; c) it has come in contact with a person, object, or thing which is out of the court; or d) it hits the top of the boards surrounding the court.

Pallino—Small object ball, sometimes called the jack or cue ball.

Spock—A throw that is thrown with sufficient velocity that it would hit the back board if it missed the target. The

spock line may be used to determine a foul.

Pointing—Throwing or rolling a ball to obtain a point close to the pallino. The roll line must be used to determine a foul.

Frame—The period in the game in which balls are played from one side of the court to the other and points awarded.

Foul-line Fouls—In both pointing and hitting, the foremost part of the specific foul-line will not be surpassed by any part of the foot before the ball leaves the player's hand. One official warning may be granted each team, after which penalties will be prescribed. The penalty for a team committing a second foul-line infraction is as follows: a) the teamed fouled against is awarded points as they were immediately preceding the foul and the frame will end. The team committing the foul will be awarded no points for the frame; or b) the fouled-against team may have the option of declining the penalty and completing the game.

Illegal Movement of a Ball Belonging to Your Own Team—If a player moves one or more of his or her team's balls, it or they are removed from the court and considered dead and play continues.

Illegal Movement of an Opponent's Ball—If a player moves one or more of his or her opponent's balls, those balls are removed and awarded one point each and play continues. Since only one team is awarded points in a frame, only the team fouled against can score points.

Illegal Movement of the Pallino by a Player—If the pallino is moved by a player, the team fouled against will be awarded as many points as the number of balls that team has already played and the frame will end. Or, the team fouled against may have the option of declining that penalty and completing the frame.

"Illegal Movement" refers to any movement of a ball by means other than the result of normal play, such as kicking, touching, etc. If a player interferes with an opponent's ball in motion, the team fouled against has the option of: a) playing the ball over; b) declaring the frame dead; or c) declining the penalty, accepting the lie of the touched ball, and continuing playing.

If a spectator, animal, or object interferes with a ball in motion and it does not touch another ball already in play, it must be played over by the same player. If a spectator, animal, or object interferes with a ball in motion and that ball touches another ball already in play, the frame is dead.

Any action that interferes with the position of a ball in play renders that frame dead.

Croquet

The object of croquet is to maneuver your ball successfully through the wickets (in the correct sequence) and be the first to hit the finishing stake. Players can be organized in one of three ways: a) two to six players playing at the same time, each with his or her own ball; b) two teams of two people, each team member playing his or her own ball; or 3) two teams of three people, each team member playing his or her own ball.

What follows are the standardized, complete rules for croquet as defined by the United States Croquet Association. To understand the rules more fully, a few definitions are in order:

Roquet—To roquet a ball is to cause your ball, by a stroke of the mallet, to come in contact with another ball, either directly or indirectly (intentionally or unintentionally).

Croquet—To strike one's own ball after placing it in contact with a roqueted ball; the player is allowed to put a foot on his or her own ball, and with the mallet, drive it against the other and send it in any direction.

Ricochet—To roquet two or more balls by one strike of the mallet.

Rover—A player who, when his or her ball has been through all of the wickets and hits the turning stake, instead of striking the starting stake (thereby finishing the game), prefers to continue to play, aiding his or her side by driving the others back.

Alive—A ball is alive once it clears a wicket, and is eligible to roquet any other ball.

Dead—After roqueting another ball, the player who roqueted is considered "dead" on that ball and cannot play off it again until his or her ball clears the next wicket.

RULES OF THE GAME

Use of the Mallet. 1) A player: a) may hold any part of the mallet handle with one or both hands and may use any stance (i.e., center, side, or golf); and b) must hit the ball (not shove or push) with a striking end of the mallet head only once per stroke (no double tap).

2) It shall be counted as a stroke if the mallet hits the wicket or ground but not the ball or misses the ball completely.

3) If a player, in attempting to strike his or her own ball, touches (with his or her foot or mallet) another ball, his or her turn ends and both balls are replaced.

4) The striker may not: a) place another mallet against a ball and then hit it with his or her own; b) move or shake a ball by hitting a wicket or stake; or c) touch or strike with his or her mallet any other ball than his or her own.

Penalty for committing a fault under rules 1, 2, 3, and 4: end of turn, with replacement of any balls having been moved.

Start of Play. 5) The toss of a coin (or lots drawn for individual play) determines the choice of order of play. A side may choose to play first or second and shall then play in the order of colors shown on the stake.

6) All balls must start from the starting tee (from one mallet head to three feet—depending upon court length) behind the first wicket with each side playing alternating turns in the rotation indicated on the stake.

Making a Wicket and Scoring Points. 7) A player whose ball passes completely through the first (or first two) wicket(s) scores the wicket point(s) and is entitled to one additional stroke. One stroke (and wicket point) earned for passing through each succeeding wicket in the order shown on page 36.

8) If a player fails to run wicket number one on his or her first stroke, his or her turn ends.

9) A ball stopping in or rolling back into the wicket has not made the wicket or scored the wicket point.

10) A ball is considered through the wicket when a straightedge placed against the approach side of the wicket does not touch the ball.

11) To score a wicket point, a ball must have started to run the wicket from the approach side.

12) A ball that is dead on another ball lying at or in the approach to the wicket may not hit that ball, and if it does the wicket is not made, the player's turn ends, and both balls are replaced.

12.a) A ball that is dead on another ball lying beyond (not intruding into) the wicket must make complete passage through the wicket, either before or after contact, to score the wicket point and receive one extra stroke.

13) A player may block (stymie) a wicket twice with a ball upon which the

opponent is dead, but on the opponent's third turn he must leave the wicket clear or be lifted and replaced after that turn. A ball that is encroaching on the direct path through a wicket is considered to be a block or stymie.

14) In the nine-wicket game a ball hitting the turning stake scores a point, clears any prior deadness, and earns one extra stroke to be played from where it comes to rest. (Not applicable in the six-wicket game.)

14.a) A rover ball hitting the finishing stake in its striker's turn (or put against it by another rover) scores the final point for that ball, which is removed from that game.

Roquet, Croquet and Extra Strokes. 15) During a turn the striker is entitled to hit (roquet) each ball (either partner's or opponent's) that his alive on and thereby earn two additional strokes. The striker's ball then becomes dead on each ball so hit and may not hit it again until he or she scores his or her next wicket point for his or her ball.

15.a) In hitting two or more balls upon which it is alive in the same stroke, the roquet will count on the first ball hit with the other being replaced.

15.b) A ball that has made a roquet cannot, in that same stroke, score a wicket point.

16) If a striker's ball hits a ball on which it is dead, the striker's turn ends and both balls are replaced.

17) A striker's ball, after making a wicket, which then hits another ball in the same stroke may elect to: a) hit (roquet) the other ball to earn two strokes; or b) not hit the other ball (and remain alive on it) and take one continuation stroke for having scored the wicket point. (The hit ball is not replaced.)

18) When a roquet is made, the striker's ball becomes a "ball-in-hand" and is brought to where the roqueted ball has come to rest in order to take the first (or croquet) stroke of two it has earned.

19) In the croquet stroke, the player may either: a) place his or her ball in contact with the roqueted ball and in striking it cause both balls to move (or shake) before taking his or her second shot; b) place his or her ball against the roqueted ball and by holding his or her ball by foot or hand drive the other away and then play his or her second shot; or c) bring his or her own ball up to a mallet's head away from the roqueted ball and play his or her two strokes from there.

20) If in the croquet stroke the player plays his or her shot from a distance greater than a mallet's head from the ball hit, or if he or she loses contact with his or her ball during a foot or hand shot, the turn is ended. All balls remain where they lie and no credit is given for wicket or stake points scored in that stroke.

21) If a ball is driven through its wicket by a ball which is alive on it in a roquet stroke or by another ball in its croquet stroke, that ball shall be counted as having scored the wicket point, is cleared of any deadness it may have had, but is not entitled to an extra stroke.

Out of Bounds. 22) A ball is out of bounds when its vertical axis crosses the boundary line (more than halfway over). It shall be replaced on the court one mallet's head from where it first went out or, if near the corner, one mallet's head from the boundary lines.

23) When a player drives his or her ball through a wicket, so that it comes to rest out of bounds, his or her turn is ended and the ball shall be placed in bounds one mallet's head from where it went out.

24) At the end of every stroke all balls except the striker's less than a mallet's head from the boundary are placed that length from the line.

24.a) If the space to which such a ball should be placed be occupied by another ball, the replaced ball shall be put up to a mallet's head in either direction from the said ball (but not touching) at the discretion of the striker.

24.b) Should two balls be sent over the boundary or less than a mallet's head from the boundary at the same place, the ball first out of bounds or closest to it is placed first with the second placed as in 24.a above.

25) If in a roquet or croquet stroke any ball (except the striker's in the roquet stroke—see rule 26) goes out of bounds, the striker's turn ends and all balls on the court remain where they lie and all balls off the court are placed one mallet's head in from the point on the boundary where they went off.

26) If, in making a roquet, the striker's ball goes out of bounds or caroms into a third ball (not the roqueted ball), sending it out, the latter ball is replaced with no penalty and the striker's ball is played as in rule 18.

27) If a ball is roqueted off the court by a striker's ball that is alive on it, the striker's turn ends but he or she remains alive on the ball so hit.

Playing Out of Turn or Wrong Ball. 28) If a ball is played out of turn, all balls are replaced as at the beginning of play, and the play is resumed in proper sequence with the offending ball losing its next turn in that sequence.

29) If a player plays the wrong ball, his or her turn ends and all balls are replaced where they were before the fault occurred. In a singles game, a striker playing the wrong ball shall be considered to have played out of turn, penalized as in rule 28.

Interference, Calling, or Condoning Faults. 30) If a ball is interfered with by an outside agent, except weather or accidentally by an opponent, in any way that materially affects the outcome of the stroke, that stroke shall be replayed. Otherwise, the ball shall be placed, as nearly as can be judged, where it would have come to rest, provided that no point or roquet can thereby be made. A rover ball prevented from scoring the stake by a staked-out ball shall be placed where it would otherwise have come to rest.

31) A fault or misplay by a player should be called as soon as it is discovered but must be called by his or her opponent before the next turn begins or else it will be automatically condoned.

Rover and Finishing the Game.
32) A player who has made all the wickets in the proper sequence becomes rover and is considered alive on all balls.

33) Assuming he or she is alive on them, a rover ball may hit any other ball only once per turn.

34) After hitting at least two balls, a rover ball may be cleared of deadness by passing through any wicket in any direction (or by hitting the turning stake in the nine-wicket game) and thus earn one continuation stroke.

35) Upon being cleared of deadness on two or three balls, a rover ball may not hit the last ball he or she was dead on until he or she hits another ball first, whereupon the temporary deadness is also cleared.

36) A rover that runs a wicket in clearing its deadness and in the same stroke hits a ball upon which it was last dead incurs no penalty, and unless either ball is driven out of bounds, both balls remain where they lie and the striker is entitled to take his or her continuation stroke.

37) A rover's ball can only be driven into the stake by its player or by another rover (either on a roquet or croquet stroke) which is alive on it, whereupon it will be considered to have finished the game (and scored a point

for itself), and shall be immediately removed from court.

38) A rover ball roqueted into the stake by a striker's ball that is dead on it shall be replaced and considered still in play.

39) A rover ball hitting the stake after making roquet is not staked out and shall play off the roqueted ball.

40) When one ball of a side (in a team game) has staked out of the game it is removed from the court immediately and play continues in the proper rotation with the staked-out ball losing all subsequent turns.

41) If in a roquet shot a striker's rover ball drives another rover ball into the stake, it is removed from play and the striker receives two strokes taken a mallet's head in any direction from the stake.

42) The game is won by the side (or player) that finishes the game with its balls (or ball) first, or in a time-limit game, by the side scoring the highest total of wicket or stake points when time expires.

Horseshoes

The following are the official playing and scoring rules as developed by National Horseshoe Pitchers Association of America:

Conduct of Players and Members. 1) No contestant, while opponent is in pitching position, shall make any remark, nor utter any sounds within the hearing of opponent, nor make any movement that does or might interfere with the opponent's playing. *Penalty:* First offense, a warning by referee; second offense, warning by referee; third offense, that game will automatically be forfeited.

1.a) Any member of the National Horseshoe Pitchers Association who

indulges in heckling or unfair rooting against any opponent in a tournament, whether with malicious intent or otherwise, shall be expelled from the grounds, and from the NHPA.

1.b) No contestant shall touch his or her own or an opponent's shoe or shoes, until a winner of point or points has been agreed upon by contestants, or decision rendered by the referee. Referee shall declare foul shoes thrown by a contestant failing to comply with his rule, and award points to the opponent, according to the position of his or her shoes.

1.c) No contestant shall walk to the opposite stake, or be informed of the position of shoes, prior to the completion of an inning.

1.d) A player, while not pitching, must remain on the opposite side of the stake of the player who is pitching, and on the rear quarter of the pitcher's platform, back of the stake. If standing back of the pitching platform the toe of one foot must remain on the rear quarter of the platform.

1.e) Any player repeatedly violating rules, or guilty of unsporting conduct, may be barred from further competition in the contest.

Foul lines. 2) Any shoe pitched while the pitcher's foot extends on or over the foul line shall be declared foul and removed from the counting distance.

2.a) In pitching the shoe, the pitcher shall stand on the pitcher's platform, at one side or other of the stake.

3) In delivering a shoe, the pitcher must remain behind the foul line until the shoe has left his or her hand.

Choice of Pitch. 4) Choice of first pitch, or follow, shall be determined by the toss of a coin or a flipped-up shoe. In successive games between the same players, loser shall choose.

Broken Shoes. 5) When a shoe lands in fair territory and is broken into separate parts, it shall be removed and the contestant allowed to pitch another shoe in its stead.

Foul Shoes. 6) Any shoe that lands outside the clay area of the opposite pitching box is a foul shoe. Any shoe that lands in fair territory but hits the backstop or other objects and comes back into the pitching area shall be called a foul shoe.

6.a) Foul shoes shall be removed from the opposite pitcher's box.

6.b) A foul shoe shall not be scored or credited except in the score column headed "shoes pitched."

6.c) When a foul shoe disrupts the position of a shoe in fair territory, the foul shoe is to be removed from the pitching area at the request of the opponent, and all other shoes are to remain as they are.

Measurements. 7) Measurements to determine points shall be made with calipers and straightedge.

SCORING RULES

There are two official methods of scoring, the cancellation method and the count-all method.

Cancellation Method. 8) A regulation game shall consist of 40 points in all contests where national title is involved. Any other contest may be decided in any manner acceptable, if national rules, constitution, and bylaws are not violated.

8.a) Game points in other tournaments, leagues, or contests may be determined by local authorities to fit their conditions.

8.b) A game is divided into innings, and each inning constitutes the pitching of two shoes by each contestant.

8.c) Score Calling Method: Scores shall be called as follows:

SCORE CALLING METHOD

No score, 4 shoes—Called as no score
    1 point—Called as 1 point
    2 points—Called as 2 points

1 ringer—Called as 1 ringer 3 points
1 ringer, 1 point—Called as 1 ringer four points
2 ringers, 6 points—Called as 2 ringers 6 points
1 ringer, each no score—Called as 1 ringer each no score
1 ringer, each 1 score—Called as 1 ringer each 1 point
3 ringers, 3 points—Called as three ringers 3 points
2 ringers, each no score—Called as two ringers each no score

In each instance, the player calling the score must call his name and must be the one scoring. In a no score situation the player pitching last shall be the one to call the score.

9) A shoe must be within six inches of the stake to score.

9.a) Closest shoe to the stake scores—1 point.

9.b) Two shoes closer than opponent's—2 points.

9.c) One ringer scores—3 points.

9.d) Two ringers—6 points.

9.e) One ringer and closest shoe of same player scores—4 points.

9.f) Party having two ringers against one for opponent scores—3 points.

9.g) All equals count as ties. If each contestant has a shoe touching the stake or each has a shoe equal distance from the stake, the closer of the two shoes will be scored as a point, if within six inches of the stake.

9.h) In case each contestant has a ringer, the next closest shoe, if within six inches, shall score—one point.

9.i) In case of tie, such as four ringers, or contestant's shoes are equal distance from the stake, causing no score for either, party pitching last in the inning will start the next inning.

9.j) A leaning shoe has no value over one touching the stake.

10) The points shall be scored according to the position of the shoes at the inning's end, that is, after the con-

testants have each thrown two shoes.

10.a) Ringer credits shall be given on the same basis.

10.b) The winner of points shall call the result. In case of a tie, the party pitching last shall call.

Definition of a Ringer. 11) A ringer is declared when a shoe encircles the stake far enough to allow the touching of both heel calks simultaneously with a straight edge, and permit a clearance of the stake.

Count-All Scoring. 12) A game shall consist of 50 shoes pitched by each player (25 innings).

12.a) Each player shall receive credit for all points according to the position of the shoes at the end of each inning, regardless of what his opponent throws. Thus it is possible for each player to score six points in any one inning. Ringers count three points and shoes within six inches of the stake count one point each.

12.b) Players shall alternate first pitch, one player having first pitch in the even innings and the other player in the odd number innings.

12.c) Ties shall be broken by pitching an extra inning or as many extra innings as are necessary to break the tie.

Double Games. 13) Two players are partners and pitch from opposite ends of the court against a similar combination of opponents. Partners' points are added together, but the individual records of ringers and shoes pitched should be kept. Otherwise the game is the same as the conventional singles or walking game.

Three-handed Games. 14) In three-handed games, when two of the players each have a ringer and a third player has no ringer, the party without a ringer is out of the scoring and others score according to conditions pertaining if only two were in the game. Otherwise, regulation rules apply.

Lawn Bowls

The following terms and rules of play are excerpted from *Official Lawn Bowls Almanac and Laws of the Game,* published by the American Lawn Bowls Association.

The Green. The green shall be a level square or rectangular area having an approved playing surface. When square, dimensions shall be 132 feet maximum, 120 feet minimum. The top surface of the retaining wall of a green on the inner side of the ditch shall be level with the surface of the green and shall be deemed for all purposes part of the green.

The Ditch. Each end of a rink shall be bounded by an excavation called the ditch. The ditch at the head end is called the front ditch, and that behind the mat, the rear ditch. Depth: Max. 8 inches, min. 2 inches below the surface of the green. Width: max. 15 inches, min. 8 inches. The walls of the ditch shall be perpendicular.

The Bank. The continuation of the outer wall of the ditch above the surface of the green is called the bank, and is the end boundary of the rink. The top of the bank shall not be less than nine inches above the surface of the green. The face of the bank shall be constructed so that a bowl or jack striking it will not be damaged. The face of the bank from the outer face of the ditch may be either vertical or may slope inward toward the green so as to overhang the outer face of the ditch no more than two inches at a point nine inches above the surface of the green. Where sod banks are used, they may slope outward from the green at an angle not to exceed 35 degrees from the perpendicular.

The Rink. A rink is the basic playing surface used during play. It shall consist of all that portion of the green and front ditch that is inside an imaginary straight line drawn between the centers of its boundary pegs or markers. Dimensions: Rectangular segment of green – Length is max. 132 feet, min. 120 feet; width is max. 19 feet, min. 14 feet.

The four corners of the rink shall be marked by pegs or markings on the bank clearly visible from the opposite end of the rink. The prepared playing surface of the green shall extend not less than two feet beyond the boundary pegs of a rink. The center line of a rink shall be indicated by a number plate located on the top of the bank at each end of the rink. Adjacent rinks shall be numbered consecutively. Pegs, discs, or other easily visible markings shall be fixed on the side banks to indicate a clear distance of 76 feet from each ditch on the line of play.

The Mat. Length: 24 inches; width: 14 inches; thickness: ¼-in. max. Material: any suitable type. When groundsheets are in use, a mat outline 24 inches long by 14 inches wide correctly and permanently marked at the rear center of a groundsheet shall be considered as the mat to which all laws apply.

The Jack. Color: white; diameter: max. $2^{17}/_{32}$ in., min. $2^{15}/_{32}$ in.; weight: max 10 oz., min. 8 oz.; material: composition or ceramic; shape: spherical.

The Bowl. Diameter: max. $5^{1}/_{8}$ in., min. $4^{5}/_{8}$ in.; metric sizes 7 to 10. Weight: no more than 3 lbs., 10 oz.; material: wood, rubber, or composition.

Measuring Devices. A standard measure shall be any type that accurately determines the result of an end.

Teams. Competition is in sides made up of one, two, three, or four players: a) singles—one against one; each player uses four bowls; b) doubles or pairs—two against two; each player uses four bowls; a team is composed of two players, lead and skip; c) triples— three against three; each player uses three bowls. (The game of triples is most commonly played in the United States.) In triples, the first player is called the "lead," the second player is known as "vice skip" (and scorer/measurer), and the third player is the team captain or "skip"; and d) fours or rinks—four against four; each player uses two bowls. For a team of four players, positions in order of play are lead, second lead (scorer), vice skip (measurer), and skip.

Duties of Team Members. Skip is the team captain and acts as the director. He or she decides disputes with opponents and carries the scorecard in a pairs match. Vice skip acts as director when skip is playing, makes necessary measurements, and determines with his or her opponent the results of an end, or, refers it to his or her skip. In a triples match, the vice skip carries the scorecard (or the skip may carry the card). The lead player places the mat as directed by the skip, unless otherwise called for by the rules. The lead delivers the jack as called for by the skip. He or she assists by directing the skip to align the jack. In a pairs match, the lead acts as vice skip.

Other duties of player acting as director: prevents disturbances of the head by an outside object; chalks his or her team's touchers, removes chalk from opponent's bowls when they are nontouchers; and guards the ditch to prevent entry of nontoucher bowl when jack and/or one or more touchers are in the ditch. Other responsibilities not specified in the laws: The lead of the team that has lost an end should retrieve the bowls in the head and place them to the right and rear of the mat.

The Match. A Match means a contest between two singles players or teams arranged to last until: a) a fixed number of shots has been scored;

2) a fixed number of ends has been played; or 3) a fixed period of time has elapsed. If an end has had at least one bowl delivered at the time limit, then the end shall be continued, but not replayed if it becomes dead.

End. End means the playing of the jack and of all bowls of both opponents in the same direction on a rink. Bowls that become or are declared "dead" are considered to have been played insofar as the end is concerned. Each end starts with delivering the jack by the first player to play. Each end is completed when the score has been agreed upon by the opponents.

Dead End. An end is declared dead whenever permitted or required by one of these laws. If, after the jack has been properly centered, action in the head disturbs the jack in a manner that causes it to come to rest beyond the boundaries of the rink, the end shall be declared dead unless the jack has been illegally disturbed and other of these laws specifically permits the jack to be replaced to its original position. A dead end shall not be counted as an end played, even though all of the balls have been delivered; it shall be replayed in the same direction unless the opponents immediately agree to the contrary.

Starting an End. Prior to the commencement of play, there shall be a toss of a coin, and the captain of the winning team shall have the right to decide who shall play first. Each succeeding end shall be started by the winner of the previous end at which a score was recorded. Succeeding ends shall be played in opposite directions. The first to play at an end that results in a dead end shall again play first at the next end.

Placing the Mat. Action in a game starts with the placement of the mat. The mat shall always be centered on the center line of the rink with the 24-inch length lengthwise of the rink, and, if

not correctly placed, the mat may be centered at any time, subject to the agreement of both skips. Otherwise the end shall be replayed.

The front end of the mat (14 inches) that is closest to the front ditch is called the mat line. All measurements from the mat shall be made from the center of the mat line.

The lead player who is to deliver the jack always places the mat. On the first end of a match, the mat must be placed so that the mat line is six feet from the ditch (see illustration). The mat shall be centered on the center line of the rink. If the mat is displaced during the course of play of an end, it shall be placed as near as possible to the original location by the next person to bowl. If out of alignment, the mat can be straightened at any time.

Following completion of the first end, the mat may be positioned any place along the center line of the rink, provided that the mat line is not less than six feet from the ditch (see illustration) or less than 76 feet from the ditch on the opposite end of the rink. At the completion of an end, it is the responsibility of the opponent of the last person to bowl to remove the mat from the green.

Delivering the Jack. The player whose turn it is to deliver the jack shall take possession of the rink. If any willful attempt be made by an opponent to divert his attention, the jack may be delivered again.

The jack shall be delivered from the mat by the first to play and it shall not be interfered with before it comes to rest while remaining within the boundary of the rink. However, the jack shall be returned and be delivered by the opponent who may relocate the mat if it comes to rest as follows: a) outside the boundary of the rink; b) in the ditch at the far end of the rink; or c) if it is not fully 70 feet from the mat line.

After one improper delivery of the jack by each player in any end, the jack shall be placed six feet from the opposite ditch, and the mat placed at the option of the first to play, provided a 70-foot or more length of the jack is maintained, and further provided that if the end being played is the first end of a match, the mat shall be placed with the mat line six feet from the rear ditch. The right of the player first delivering the jack in that end to play the first bowl shall not be affected.

Any player on the rink may challenge the length a jack has been delivered before the first bowl is delivered, subject in the case of a team, to the approval of his or her captain.

The jack shall be placed on the center line of the rink and as nearly as is practical, equal with the distance it was delivered, except that, when delivered to less than six feet from the front ditch, the jack shall be placed six feet from the front ditch. If the length of the jack is challenged before it is aligned, and all or a portion of the jack is at least 70 feet from the mat line, it shall be aligned by swinging on an arc so that it remains the same distance from the center of the mat line.

If the jack is interfered with before coming to rest within the boundary of the rink: a) by an opposing player or by the maker, or by any other outside influence, it shall be delivered again by the same player, or b) by a teammate of the lead delivering the jack, it shall be delivered again by his opponent who may relocate the mat.

Directing a Player. The director may assist a player by placing an object above the green for guidance (a hat, cap, towel, etc.), but such objects must be withdrawn from the position indicated before the bowl is delivered. Also, at no time shall either the jack or a bowl be touched while a player is being directed. Each director, while in possession of the rink, may stand anywhere in the head while directing his player, but shall retire to a position behind the jack as soon as the bowl is delivered.

Location of Players on the Rink. All players at the mat end of the rink, except the one who has position of the mat, shall not be less than five feet behind the mat line. All players at the head end of the rink, except the director in possession of the rink, shall be not less than six feet behind the jack. All players on both teams at the head end of the rink shall remain motionless from the time the player takes his stance on the mat until he delivers his bowl.

Possession of the Rink. The player whose turn it is to deliver the bowl, together with his director, shall have possession of the rink as soon as the previously delivered bowl has come to rest, except for the time allowed to mark a toucher. The player in possession of the rink shall be allowed to receive instructions and to deliver his bowl without interference. Any communication between the head end and the mat end of the rink by opponents during this period shall be deemed interference.

Delivery. A bowl is delivered when it leaves the hand of the player on the mat while performing his normal delivery motion, provided it passes the mat line. A player may carry his bowl beyond the mat line without penalty.

Bowl in Course. A bowl in course means a bowl from the time of its delivery until it comes completely to rest.

Foot Faulting. A player shall take his stance on the mat with one or both feet entirely within the confines of the mat and, at the time of delivering his bowl, one foot must be on or over the confines of the mat. Any delivery not in accordance with this law shall constitute foot faulting, in which case: a) the

player shall be warned and the bowl may be stopped and declared dead by the umpire, and b) if such a dead bowl is not stopped and, while in course touches any portion of the head, the opponent shall immediately remove the dead bowl and decide whether the head shall be reset, shall remain as disturbed, or whether the end shall be dead.

Playing Someone Else's Bowl. If a player delivers a bowl other than his own, it shall be allowed to come to rest. It should then be replaced at that spot with a correct bowl.

Playing Prematurely. If a bowl is delivered before the previously delivered bowl comes to rest, it may be stopped by direction of the opposing director. It shall then be returned to the mat and replayed. If not stopped, it is allowed as a properly delivered bowl.

Omitting to Play. A player who has neglected to play a bowl in proper sequence shall forfeit the right to play such bowl if a bowl has been played by each team. If the result of an end has been agreed upon or the head has been touched in the agreed process of scoring the end, then a player who has omitted to play a bowl shall forfeit the right to play it. The skip who is last to play in any end may decline to play his last bowl by so stating to the opposing skip and requesting that the head be counted.

Prompt Playing. If a player fails to deliver his bowl within two minutes of the coming to rest of his opponent's previously delivered bowl, he shall forfeit the right to play that bowl during that end, and the match shall proceed as though he had accepted his turn.

Order of Playing. The order of delivery shall alternate between the opponents with each bowl played. If a player delivers a bowl out of his turn, it should be stopped by either director or by the marker (on the request of either player)

and be replayed in its correct order. If it is not stopped, and comes to rest without having touched any portion of the head, it shall be returned to the mat and replayed in its correct order. If it is not stopped and, while in course, touches any portion of the head, the opponent shall immediately decide whether the head shall remain as disturbed, and the opponent shall play two successive bowls to restore the correct sequence. If, before the mistake is noticed, a bowl has been delivered in the reversed order, the opponent shall then play two successive bowls to restore the correct sequence.

Starting an End. Prior to the commencement of play, there shall be a toss of a coin, and the captain of the winning team shall have the right to declare who shall play first. Each succeeding end shall be started by the winner of the previous end at which a score was recorded. Succeeding ends shall be played in opposite directions, unless the previous end was a dead end, in which case it shall be replayed in the same direction unless the opponents immediately agree to the contrary. The first to play at an end that results in a dead end shall again play first at the next end.

Placing the Mat. The mat shall always be centered on the center line of the rink with the 24-inch side lengthwise of the rink, and, if not correctly placed, the mat may be centered at any time, subject to the agreement of both skips. Otherwise the end shall be replayed. The front end of the mat (14 inches) that is closest to the front ditch is called the Mat Line. All measurements from the mat line shall be made from the center of the mat line. At the first end of each match, the mat line shall be six feet from the rear ditch. (Whenever ground sheets are in use, this rule shall apply to the first and all subsequent ends.) At all subsequent ends, the mat may be placed in any position along the center line of the rink, provided the mat line is not less than six feet from the rear ditch or less than 76 feet from the front ditch. The mat shall be placed by the first to play for that end and shall not be moved during the remainder of the end, except as permitted or required otherwise.

Displacement of Mat. If the mat be displaced during the progress of an end, it shall be replaced as nearly as is practical in the same position by the next play. If the mat is out of alignment with the center line of the rink, it may be straightened at any time during the end.

Removal of Mat. The responsibility for the removal of the mat and the conclusion of an end shall rest with the opponent of the last player.

Delivering the Jack. The player whose turn it is to deliver the jack shall take possession of the rink. The jack shall be delivered from the mat by the first to play and it shall not be interfered with before it comes to rest while remaining within the boundary of the rink. (If any willful attempt is made by an opponent to divert his attention, the jack may be delivered again.) However, the jack shall be returned and be delivered by the opponent who may relocate the mat if it comes to rest as follows: a) wholly outside the rink boundary, b) in the front ditch, or c) with no portion at least 70 feet from the mat line before or after being aligned.

After one improper delivery of the jack by each player in any end, the jack shall be placed six feet from the opposite ditch, and the mat placed at the option of the first to play, provided a 70-foot or more length of the jack is maintained, and further provided that if the end being played is the first end of a match, the mat shall be placed with the mat line six feet from the rear ditch.

The right of the player first delivering the jack in that end to play the first bowl shall not be affected.

The jack shall be placed on the center line of the rink and as nearly as is practical, equal with the distance it was delivered (except that, when delivered to less than six feet from the front ditch, the jack shall be placed six feet from the front ditch). Any player on the rink may challenge the length a jack has been delivered before the first bowl is delivered, subject in case of a team to the approval of his captain. If the length of the jack is challenged before it is aligned, and all or a portion of the jack is at least 70 feet from the mat line, it shall be aligned by swinging on an arc so that it remains the same distance from the center of the mat line.

If a jack is interfered with before coming to rest within the boundary of the rink by an opposing player by the marker, or by any other outside influence, it shall be delivered again by the same player. If the jack is interfered with by a teammate of the lead delivering the jack, it shall be delivered again by his opponent who may relocate the mat as permitted.

Directing a Player. The director may assist a player by placing an object above the green for guidance, but such object shall be withdrawn from the position indicated before the bowl is delivered. At no time shall either the jack or a bowl be touched while directing a player. Each director, while in possession of the rink, may stand anywhere in the head while directing his player but shall retire to a position behind the jack as soon as the bowl is delivered.

Location of Players on Rink. All players at the mat end of the rink shall be not less than five feet behind the mat line, except the player in possession of the rink. All players at the head end of the rink shall be not less than six feet

behind the jack, except the director who is in possession of the rink. All players at the head end of the rink on both teams shall remain motionless from the time an opponent takes his stance on the mat until the bowl is delivered.

Possession of the Rink. The player whose next turn it is to deliver his bowl, and his director, shall have possession of the rink after the previously delivered bowl has come to rest, except for time allowed to mark a toucher. The player in possession of the rink shall be allowed to receive instructions and to deliver his bowl without interference. Any communication between the head end and the mat end of the rink by opponents during this period shall be deemed interference.

Delivery. A bowl is delivered when it leaves the hand of the player on the mat while performing his normal delivery motion, provided it passes the mat line. A player may not carry his bowl beyond the mat line without penalty.

Bowl in Course. A bowl is in course from the time of its delivery until it comes completely to rest.

Foot Faulting. A player shall take his stance on the mat with one or both feet entirely within the confines of the mat and, at the time of delivering his bowl, one foot must be on or over the confines of the mat. Any delivery not in accordance with this law shall constitute foot faulting. If the umpire be of the opinion that a player is foot faulting, he shall warn the player so offending. The umpire may, after having given a warning, have the bowl stopped and declared dead. If such a dead bowl is not stopped and, while in course, touches any portion of the head, the opponent shall immediately remove the dead bowl and decide whether the head shall rest, shall remain as disturbed, or whether the end shall be dead.

Playing Another's Bowl. If a player, in his turn, delivers a bowl other than his own, it shall be allowed to complete its course. When the incorrect bowl comes to rest, it shall be replaced with a correct bowl by the opponent or by the marker, if so requested.

Playing Prematurely. If a bowl is delivered while the preceding bowl is still in course, the first mentioned bowl may be stopped by the opposing director, or by the marker on direction from the opponent, returned to the mat and replayed. However, if it is not stopped, it shall be deemed a correctly delivered bowl.

Omitting to Play. A player, who has neglected to play a bowl in proper sequence, shall forfeit the right to play such bowl if a bowl has been played by each team. If the result of an end has been agreed upon or the head has been touched in the agreed process of scoring the end, then a player who has omitted to play a bowl shall forfeit the right to play it. The skip to last play in any end may decline to play his last bowl by so stating to the opposing skip and requesting that the head be counted.

Declining to Play Promptly. If a player fails to deliver his bowl within two minutes of the coming to rest of his opponent's previously delivered bowl, he shall forfeit the right to play that bowl during that end, and the match shall proceed as though he had accepted his turn.

Bowl in Course Outside the Rink. A bowl in course, delivered on the *wrong* bias, which leaves the rink over a side boundary shall be dead regardless of where it comes to rest. A bowl in course, delivered on the *correct* bias, which leaves the rink over a side boundary shall: a) continue in play, if it comes to rest on the rink from which it was delivered without touching another object when in course; b) be

dead, if it comes to rest wholly outside of the rink from which it was delivered without touching another object while in course; c) be replayable if it collides with any person or object or is stopped to avoid such a collision while in course outside of the rink from which it was delivered.

Collisions. If a bowl or jack coming from an adjacent rink or driven from an adjacent rink collides with a bowl in course on the rink in play, the bowl in course shall be returned to the mat and replayed.

Dead Bowl. In addition to other aforementioned conditions, a bowl also becomes dead under the following conditions not covered elsewhere: a) if a bowl in course comes to rest with the entire bowl less than 45 feet from the center of the mat line; b) if, not being a toucher, it rebounds from the face of the bank back onto the green; c) if, not being a toucher, it falls into the front ditch; d) if it passes the end boundary of the rink.

Touchers. A toucher is a bowl that, while in course, touches the jack or falls over and touches the jack before the next bowl has been delivered while jack is on the playing surface of the rink. No bowl can be accounted a toucher by playing onto or coming in contact with the jack while the jack is in the front ditch.

Chalking. A toucher is distinguished by a chalk mark placed on the bowl, either by the marker or the director of the team to which it belongs, before the next delivered bowl has come to rest. If not so marked, it shall not be regarded as a toucher except that, if either director feels that chalking a toucher is likely to move the ball or alter the head, such a bowl may be "indicated a toucher" and play continued on that basis. The same ruling also applies to removing an improper chalk mark from a nontoucher bowl, which may be indi-

cated a "nontoucher."

If the chalk mark is not removed from a bowl before it is delivered at the next end, such mark shall be removed by the opposing director or marker as soon as the bowl comes to rest. If a toucher be moved when being chalked or when removing an improper chalk mark by the marker, it shall be immediately replaced by him. If a toucher is moved when being chalked or when an improper chalk is being removed by a director, it shall be immediately replaced by his opposing director.

Rebounding From the Face of the Bank. If a toucher rebounds from the face of the bank back onto or touching the boundary of the rink, it shall remain as part of the head and continue in play. If the head is disturbed by a rebounding toucher, the head shall remain as so disturbed.

In the Ditch. If a toucher comes to rest in the front ditch and any portion is within or touching the boundary of the rink, it shall remain as part of the head and continue in play. If a ditched jack and/or toucher is disturbed by another toucher entering the front ditch, the head shall remain as so disturbed. The position of a toucher in the ditch may be marked by placing a suitable object on the bank above it, never on the surface of the rink.

Movement of Touchers. A toucher in play in the ditch may be moved by the impact of a jack in play or of another toucher in play, and also by the impact of a nontoucher that remains in play after the impact, and any movement of the toucher by such incidents shall be valid. However, should the non-toucher enter the ditch after the impact, it shall be dead, and the toucher in the ditch shall be deemed to have been displaced by a dead bowl and the provisions under *"Disturbance at Play"* shall apply.

Moved or Ditched Jack. If, by the effect of the play, the jack is moved to a different location on the rink or into the front ditch and any portion of the jack remains within or touching the boundary of the rink, it shall remain as part of the head and continue in play. A jack in the front ditch may be moved by the impact of a toucher in play and also by the impact of a nontoucher that remains in play after the impact; any movements of the jack by such incidents shall be valid. However, should the nontoucher enter the ditch after impact, it shall be dead and the jack shall be deemed to have been displaced by a dead bowl and the provisions under *Disturbance at Play* shall apply. The position of a ditched jack still in play may be marked by placing a suitable object on the bank above it, never on the playing surface of the rink.

Rebounding Jack. If, by the effect of play, the jack rebounds from the face of the bank back onto or touching the boundary of the rink, it shall remain as part of the head and continue in play. If, by the effect of play, the jack rebounds toward the mat and the jack comes to rest less than 66 feet from the mat line, the end shall be dead.

Jack Embedded in the Bank. If, by the effect of play, the jack becomes embedded in the face of the bank wholly above the level of the green, the end shall be dead. If, by the effect of play, the jack becomes embedded in the face of the bank or the wall of the ditch, so that any portion of the jack is below the level of the green and within the boundary of the rink, it shall remain as part of the head and continue in play.

Damaged Jack. If, by the effect of play or other cause, the jack is damaged sufficiently to affect the result of an end, the end shall be dead.

Disturbance by a Player. If the jack or a bowl is interfered with or disturbed by any player while it is in motion or at rest on the green or in the front ditch, the opposing captain shall have the option to: a) have the disturbed jack or bowl replaced as nearly as practicable to its original position; b) permit the jack or bowl to remain in the disturbed position and continue play; c) declare a disturbed bowl dead, remove from green and continue play; or d) declare the end dead. The chalking of or the removing of a chalk mark on a bowl shall *not* constitute a disturbance thereof. The lifting of a bowl that is at rest and is likely to be disturbed by a bowl in course on its correct bias from an adjoining rink shall *not* be deemed to be deliberate disturbance.

Disturbance by Play. If the head toward which the bowl is delivered is disturbed by the bowl in course, the head shall remain as disturbed except if the head is disturbed by a bowl in course that has been deflected by outside influence (see *Outside Disturbance*).

If the head is disturbed by the jack or a toucher bowl entering the front ditch or rebounding from the face of the bank back onto the green, the head shall remain as so disturbed. If the head be disturbed by a nontoucher bowl entering the front ditch or rebounding from the face of the bank back onto the green, the jack and/or bowl(s) so disturbed shall be immediately replaced by the opposing director or singles player, whose decision is final. In a singles match, the marker may assist the opposing player in replacing the disturbed jack and/or bowl(s), but the final decision rests with the player.

Outside Disturbance. If the umpire or marker, when measuring the result of an end, moves either the jack or bowl being measured, he shall declare that particular measurement a tie.

If any part of the head is moved or interfered with by any neutral person or by an object from outside the rink, the jack or bowl(s) shall be replaced by agreement between the opponents, or failing an agreement, the end shall be dead. However, if the measures have already agreed on one or more points for a particular team and are in the process of determining the next point, that agreement on points shall stand.

Measuring on Completion of an End. Measurements shall be made to the nearest point of each object, preferably using an approved measuring devise that must be securely locked while measuring. Special conditions are: a) when measuring between a jack or bowl in the front ditch and a jack or bowl on the surface of the green, a flexible tape or line must be used. Such measurements must be made directly over the edge of the rink to the nearest points on the jack and bowl being measured; and b) calipers and other rigid measuring devises are permissible only when the jack and all bowls being measured are on the same plane.

Premature Measuring. No measuring shall be allowed until the end has been completed. If a player deliberately measures by placing any object or part of his body between the jack and the bowl before the completion of an end, the opposing captain shall have the option to: a) continue play without penalty; b) declare dead all such improperly measured bowls that belong to the player or team making the measurement, remove such dead bowls from the rink and continue play; or c) declare the end dead.

Obstructed Measure. If the determination as to whether any bowl shall score as shot is hindered or prevented by reason of its resting on another bowl, the bowl to be measured shall be suitably secured in its position and the obstructing bowl removed.

Determining the Result. When the end is completed, or deemed to be completed, the opponents shall agree on the result, and such agreement shall be final. Neither the jack nor bowls shall be moved until each director has agreed to the number of shots, except as for under *obstructed measure.* Either director may invoke a delay of 30 seconds from the time the last delivered bowl has come to rest before counting the head. If the opponents are unable to agree, the result shall be determined by the umpire, or in a singles match, by the marker, if so requested by both opponents.

Scoring. The player or team having the nearest bowl to the jack shall score one shot and an additional one shot for every other bowl that is nearer to the jack than the nearest bowl of his opponent.

The Ends. If the nearest bowls of the opponents are equidistant from the jack, no score shall be recorded for that end, but the end shall be counted as an end played in a match of a fixed number of ends, unless the specific, published conditions of the match provide that it shall not count as an end played. In the event of a tie end, the two skips involved shall toss a coin to determine control of the jack on the next end.

The Match Scores. If the total number of shots scored by each opponent is equal at the conclusion of a match, the match shall result in a tie, unless the conditions of the contest require a winner. If a winner is required, an additional end shall be played. The opponents shall toss a coin and the winner of the first toss shall have the option to decide who shall play first.

Shuffleboard

The following rules of play are excerpted from *Official Rules of the National Shuffleboard Association, Inc.,* revised edition, 1991.

Players. The game of shuffleboard is played by either two persons (called singles) or by four persons (called doubles).

Object. The object of the game is to propel discs by means of a cue onto the scoring diagram at the opposite end of the court—to score, to prevent an opponent from scoring, or both.

Discs. Discs shall be made of composition not less than 9/16 inches and not more than one inch in thickness, six inches in diameter, and not less than 11.5 ounces in weight. New discs shall weigh 15 ounces. Four discs shall be colored red, four colored black. These eight discs comprise a set. (Other color combinations may be used, as white or yellow, in place of red.) Care should be taken that all discs in a set shall be uniform in weight and thickness.

Cue. The cue shall not have an overall length of more than six feet, three inches. No metal parts on the cue shall touch playing surface of court.

Condition. Players shall not be required to play with discs, new or old, that are not in satisfactory condition. Defective discs will be replaced by good discs, if available. Any change of discs must be made before the practice round begins. New discs are not to be used in tournament play, unless thoroughly broken in.

PLAYING RULES

Assigning Disc Colors. The player or team with the lowest chart line number will play the first game with red (or yellow) discs, then change color and play the second game with black discs.

Color choice for the third game is determined by two opposing players shooting from the head of the court to the far deadline, shooting alternately, first red then black. The first three discs of each player are for practice and shall be removed progressively. The last disc shot by each player shall be left on the court. The disc nearer to the far deadline (lag line) determines who shall have color choice. Measurement is made from the center of the disc to the center of the line. If the last (fourth) black disc shot touches the red disc, color choice goes to the player of red. In doubles, partners shall play on the same color at both ends of the court.

Court Positions. In doubles, each team may change ends of court once immediately, or before practice rounds begin. The team playing red discs must make the first decision to change ends.

Practice. Before practice begins, each player may shoot two discs to check the speed of the court. Two full rounds of practice on assigned color are allowed before the first and second games. If a third game is necessary, no practice is allowed before the third game.

Order of Play. To start a game, the red disc is shot first. Play alternates, red then black—until all of the discs are shot. Red shall always be played from the right side of the head of the court, and the left side of the foot of the court.

In singles, after all discs are played, constituting a half-round, the players walk to the opposite end of the court, or foot of the court, and start play, with color lead changing to black. In doubles, after all discs are played at head of court, play starts at foot or opposite end—red leading, black following. Color lead does *not* change until both ends have been played (a round).

The second game is started by the red at the head of the court. The third game is started by the red at the head of the court.

Error in Color Lead. An error in color lead shall be corrected—the half round is played over with correct color lead—if discovered before a half round is completed; otherwise, play continues in the order started at the beginning of the game.

Placing the Discs. Players shall place their four discs within and not touching the lines of their respective half of the 10-Off area. (Penalty: 5-Off—not applied to the player until he has played a disc.) Discs must be played from the clear within the respective half of a 10-Off area.

Disc Penalties. If a disc played touches the front or back line, there is a penalty of 5-Off. If a disk played touches side or triangle, there is a penalty of 10-Off; offender's disc is removed, and opponent is credited with any of his discs replaced.

Displaced Discs. All displaced discs shall be removed from the court immediately after scoring of opponent's displaced discs. Any 10-Offs the offender had on the court that were displaced will be removed before further play and also deducted from offender's score.

Disc Touching Lines. It is common practice for players to jockey or slide the playing disc backward and forward to see if there is sand that might interfere with the disc sliding evenly. No penalty is to be called on this practice if lines are touched or crossed while jockeying. Discs in motion may cross outside diagonal line.

Discs in Play. A disc is played when it is completely in the seven area, but when the disc stops between the farthest dead line and the seven area, it is a dead disc and shall be removed from further play. If a disc is touching the farthest dead line, it is in play.

Baseline. A player shall not step on or over the baseline of the court, or an extension of the baseline, except to gather and place his discs (penalty: 5-Off for this offense when not in the act of executing a shot.)

Players must not touch a foot, hand, knee, or any other part of their body to the court on or over the baseline or extension of the baseline at any time while executing a shot (penalty: 10-Off).

Players must stand behind the baseline extension in the alley between the courts, but not on adjoining court, before or while shooting (penalty: 5-Off).

The area between the baseline of the court and an imaginary line, even with the back of the bench, and bounded on the sides by the farthest line of each adjoining alley, should be considered part of the court.

Player Positioning. In doubles, players must remain seated when play is to their end of the court until all discs are shot, the score is announced, and the official has called "Play" or signalled or otherwise authorized them to do so (penalty: 5-Off).

In singles, players must not cross the baseline to proceed to the other end of the court until the official has called "Play" or signaled or otherwise authorized them to do so (penalty: 5-Off).

Players must not leave the court during a game without permission, except to gather discs at the end of a half round (penalty: 10-Off). There is no penalty if a player leaves the court between games; however, players may not be gone for more than 10 minutes (penalty: 10-Off). A game is concluded when the referee announces the score, the score is recorded on the scoreboard, and the scores are recorded on the player's card. The referee on the court shall start the time when the game is concluded.

Player Behavior. Players shall not stand in the way of, or have cue in the way of, or interfere with opponent while he or she is executing a play (penalty: 5-Off). Players shall not touch live discs at any time (penalty: 10-Off, and that round played over). Players shall not talk or make remarks to disconcert opponent's play (penalty: 10-Off). Any remarks or motions to a partner that indicate coaching is prohibited (penalty: 10-Off).

A player may not shoot before an opponent's disc comes to rest (penalty: 10-Off, the offender's disc removed, and opponent is credited with any of his discs that were displaced). All displaced discs shall be removed from the court immediately after scoring of opponent's displaced discs. Any 10-Off the offender had on the court that was displaced will be removed before further play, and also be deducted from the offender's score. If a player intentionally delays or stalls, there is a penalty: 5-Off.

If a cue slips from a player's hand and couches or displaces any live disc, the player is penalized 10-Off and the opponent is credited with any of his or her discs that were displaced, and that half round shall be played over unless game point has been reached by the offender's opponent. If the cue does not touch or displace any live disc, there is no penalty.

Hesitation Shots. Forward motion of the cue and disc must be continuous or accelerated. Any 10-Offs that the offender had on the court that were displaced will be removed before further play and also be deducted from the offender's score.

Hook Shots. The shot must be delivered in a straight line with continuous forward motion of cue and disc. Penalty: 10-Off, offender's disc removed, and opponent credited with score of any of his discs that were displaced. All displaced discs shall be removed from the court immediately after scoring of opponent's displaced discs. Any 10-Offs the offender had on the court that were displaced will be removed from further play, and also be deducted from the offender's score.

Consecutive Discs. If a player shoots two consecutive discs, there is a penalty: 10-Off, plus any 10-Offs the offender may have on the court. Other good discs of offender will not count. Opponent is credited with all good discs on the court before second disc was played (except 10-Off), and that half round is played over unless game point has been reached by offender's opponent.

Dead Discs. A disc or discs returning or remaining on the playing area of the court, after having struck any object outside the playing area, shall be removed from further play. They are called dead discs.

If a dead disc rebounds and touches a live disc, or causes another dead disc to touch a live disc, the half round shall be played over. A penalty of 10-Off will be assessed of the player shooting the offending disc that causes the replay—unless it was the last disc (the eighth disc) played in the half round. Then, that half round is not replayed, and the score that was on the court immediately before the rebound shall count.

If a dead disc coming from another court moves a live disc, that half round shall be played over with no score credited to any player. A penalty of 5-Off will be assessed the player shooting the offending disc causing the replay. Note: it shall be the responsibility of the host club to install proper backstops (preferably two-by-twos loosely anchored), to prevent rebounds.

Any disc that clearly leaves the court beyond the farthest baseline, or goes off the side of the court, is a dead disc. A disc that stops less than eight inches beyond the farthest baseline shall be removed. A disc that is leaning over the edge of the court and touch-ing the alley shall be immediately removed.

When a player's disc jumps over the backstop, or causes another disc to jump over the backstop, a penalty of 10-Off will be assessed of the player shooting the offending disc. Special consideration may be given in this situation when court conditions are such that they render this rule impractical or unfair to the players.

SCORING

Scoring Diagram. One 10-point area, two 8-point areas, two 7-point areas, and one 10-Off point area. After both players have shot their four discs, score all discs on the diagram within and not touching the lines; separation triangle in 10-Off area is not considered. When judging a disc in relation to lines, the official shall sight directly down.

Mounted Disc. A mounted disc, or a disc resting on top of another, happens sometimes when players use excessive force in shooting. Each disc shall be judged according to scoring rules.

Game Point. Play continues until all discs have been shot in the half round, even if game point has been reached.

Tie Games. If a tie game results at game point or over, play is continued in regular rotation of play, until two full rounds in doubles or one full round in singles are completed. At that time, the side with the higher score wins, even if it has less than 75 points or the number of points specified as game points. If the score is tied again, play continues again as outlined above.

Scoring Errors. If a scoring error occurs at the end of a half round and it is discovered before the next half round is completed, the error must be corrected. Otherwise, the score as shown on the scoreboard must stand, unless both sides agree on the correction.

VIOLATIONS AND PENALTIES

Discs not in starting area	5-Off
Discs touching front or back line	5-Off
Played disc touching side of triangle	10-Off
Player stepping on or over baseline or extension while not in the act of shooting	5-Off
Player stepping on or over baseline or extension while in the act of shooting	10-Off
Player standing or stepping on adjoining court, except to gather disc	5-Off
Player not remaining seated	5-Off
Player leaving court without permission during game	10-Off
Player leaving court between games and being gone for more than 10 minutes	10-Off
Player standing in way of, or equipment in way of, opponent	5-Off
Player touching live disc	10-Off
Player making remarks to disconcert opponent	10-Off
Player making remark or motion to partner	10-Off
Player shooting disc while opponent's disc is in motion	10-Off
Player intentionally stalling	5-Off
Player's cue slipping from hand and contacting live disc	10-Off
Hesitation shot	10-Off
Hook shot	10-Off
Player shooting two consecutive discs	10-Off
Improper action not otherwise covered	10-Off
Rebounding dead discs touching live disc	10-Off
Disc coming from another court	5-Off
Moving disputed disc before inspection	10-Off
Appealing without reason	10-Off

Outdoor Volleyball

The following rules of play are excerpted from the *Official United States Volleyball Rule Book, 1992*, published by the United States Volleyball Association.

The official United States volleyball rules shall govern play on beaches and grass except for the following exceptions extracted from the Federation Internationale de Volleyball Rules, 1989-1992 edition, and approved by the FIVB World Beach Volleyball Council. Some areas have been using rules based on the Association of Volleyball Professionals (AVP) rules and the Women's Professional Volleyball Association (WPVA) rules. Where the rules differ, a note to that effect is included.

Playing Area. The playing court shall be 18 m long by 9 m wide (59' X 29' 6").

It is the responsibility of players to assure that lines are in their proper location prior to the start of each play. If lines become misplaced during play, play shall continue. The referee will make decisions based on the original location of the line. If the referee cannot make a decision, a playover will be directed.

Playing Area Clearance: There shall be a clear space around the court of at least 3 m (9' 10") in each direction. The space above the playing area shall be free of obstructions. The playing surface shall be reasonably level and may consist of either sand or grass free of rocks, shells, or other items which could cause injury to players.

Note: Under AVP rules, a clear area of 3 meters on the sides and 5 meters on the end of the courts should surround an outdoor court.

Grass courts should not contain sprinkler heads. Any sprinkler heads, holes, or uneven areas on the court must be made safe for players.

Sand courts must have a consistent layer of fine-grained sand and should be at least 50 cm in depth to prevent player contact of the surface beneath the court.

Boundary Lines and Markings. Boundary lines shall be made of rope or other material having the same characteristics as rope and of a color that is in contrast to the color of the surface being used for play. Anchors for boundary lines shall be installed in such a manner that they will not cause injury or cause player to trip.

The Center Line. The center line is not marked. The plane of the net serves as an invisible unmarked centerline dividing the court into two team areas.

Service Area. The width of the service area is limited by the imaginary extension of the side boundary lines and extends in depth to the nearest obstacle.

Attack Lines. Attack lines* are used for 6 players, mixed six or reverse mixed six competition only. Attack lines must be marked or secured in such a manner as to not cause player injury. Three-meter attack lines may be marked by using non-toxic white powder, whitewash, chalk tape or a thin elastic line secured at the boundary lines 3 m from the net.

*Definition of attack lines is as follows: In each team area a line 5 cm (2") wide shall be drawn between the sidelines parallel to the center line and 3 m (9' 10") from the middle of the center line to the rearmost edge of the attack line. The attack area, limited by the center line and the attack line extends indefinitely beyond the sidelines.

Substitution Zones. There are no designated substitution zones for outdoor competition. In competitions where substitutions are authorized, exchanges of players should be made near the net.

Minimum Temperature. The temperature should be compatible for outdoor competition. The wind chill factor should not be below 10 degrees C. (50 degrees F.)

THE NET

The net shall be not less than 9.50 m (32') in length and 1 m (39") in width throughout the full length when stretched. Nets for outdoor play must contain a 5-cm-wide horizontal band at both the top and bottom of the net. The bands may be of any color (preferably dark blue) and may contain logos or other type of printing.

The net must be constructed of 10 cm (4") square dark mesh ony. A flexible cable or cord with a minimum breaking strength 1364 kg (3000 lb) shall be stretched through the top tape and a flexible cable or cord having a minimum breaking strength of 455 kg (1000 lb) through the lower tape of the net. The ends of the net should be capable of receiving a wooden dowel to keep each end of the net in a straight line when tight.

Net Height. The height of the net measured from the center of the court shall be 2.43 m (7' 11") for men and 2.24 m (7' 4") for women. the two ends of the net must be at the same height from the playing surface and cannot exceed the regulation height by more than 2 cm (¾").

Vertical Tape Markers. White material 5 cm (2") wide and 1 m (39") in length shall be fastened to the net at each end over and perpendicular to the corresponding sideline. The vertical tape markers are considered to be part of the net.

Net Supports. Net supports may be made of either wood or metal and shall be of a constitution so as not to allow bending when net tension is applied. They must be free of hazardous extrusions (nails, splinters, etc.). Bolts, or other protrusions which cannot be removed, must be padded. Guy wires securing portable net supports must be made of bright colors or marked with flags. Anchors for guy wires and boundary lines must be driven flush to the playing surface and be of such design as to be free of any sharp edges.

Antennas. The net support poles serve as imaginary antennas for outdoor play. A ball crossing the net between the net supports remains in play.

Note: If the net becomes significantly displaced during play, or if the net becomes significantly lowered, play shall be stopped and a replay directed when the net location and/or height has been corrected.

THE BALL

The ball shall be spherical with a laceless leather or leatherlike water-resistant cover of 18 panels covering a rubberlike bladder. The pressure of the ball shall be 5.0 lbs./sq. in. Balls may be white, solid color, or multi-colored.

Official Ball for Match. Teams must agree upon the ball to be used. If there is a disagreement, each team will provide a ball that the referee deems suitable for play. A coin toss will then be conducted to determine which ball will be used.

RIGHTS AND DUTIES OF PLAYER AND TEAM PERSONNEL

Rules of the Game. Players must know and abide by the Official Sand and Grass Volleyball Rules.

Time-Out Requests. Each team is permitted two time-outs of one minute duration each per game. In addition, each team may be granted four sand time-outs of 15 seconds per game.

Note: Additional time-outs may be requested and granted. Excess time-outs cause the team to be sanctioned with a side-out or awarding of a point to the opponents.

Sand time-outs: AVP and WPVA rules permit sand time-outs to be of 20 seconds duration.

Player Conduct. Participants may be sanctioned by the first referee for misconduct for the following acts: a) addressing officials concerning their decisions; b) making profane or vulgar acts, gestures or remarks; c) committing acts or gestures tending to influence officials; d) disruptive coaching or other actions by any team member; e) crossing the vertical plane of the net with any part of the body with the purpose of distracting an opponent while the ball is in play.

Degree of Individual Sanctions. Offenses committed by team members may result in the following sanctions by the first referee: a) Warning: For minor unsporting offenses such as talking to opponents, spectators or officials, shouting or other minor unsporting acts that disrupt the conduct of the game, a warning (yellow card) is issued and is recorded on the scoresheet. A second minor offense during the same game by the same team member must result in a penalty (red card); b) Penalty: For rude behavior, a second minor offense or other serious offenses, a penalty (red card) is issued by the first referee and is recorded on the scoresheet. A penalty automatically entails the loss of service by the offending team if serving, or if not serving, the awarding of a point to the opponents. A second act warranting the issuing of a penalty to a team member during the same game results in expulsion; c) Expulsion: Extremely offensive conduct (such as obscene or insulting words or gestures) toward officials, spectators, or other players results in expulsion of a team member from the game (red and yellow cards together) in which the offense occurred. Expelled individuals must leave the court and team area until the next game of the match. A second expulsion during a match must result in the disqualification of the team

member(s). No further penalty is assessed; d) Disqualification: A second expulsion during a match, or any feigned, attempted, or actual physical aggression toward an official, spectator, or opponent results in the disqualification of the team member for the remainder of a match (red and yellow cards held apart). A disqualified team member must leave the area (including spectator area) of the match. No further penalty is assessed.

Misconduct Between Games. Any sanctions for misconduct between games will be administered in the game following such misconduct.

Lineup Checks. A team may request the scorekeeper to give the name of its player who should be serving. No information will be provided about the opponent's lineup. In doubles play, either player may request lineup information about their team.

Teams. Competition may consist of:

a) 2-person (Doubles) two players per team

b) 3-person (Triples) three players per team

c) 4-person (Quads) four players per team

d) 6-person (Regular) six players per team

Composition of Teams. Teams must consist of equal numbers of players on each team. Teams comprised of both male and female players must contain equal numbers of males and females on each team. All mixed six competition may be played with regular or reverse Co-Ed rules.

Uniforms. Uniforms may consist of neat and clean shorts or bathing suit. Jerseys or tank tops are optional unless specified in tournament rules. Jerseys or shorts must be numbered on the front. There is no requirement for players to wear identical uniforms. It is permissible for players to wear hats or visors and sunglasses. It is not a fault if such items fall off during play and contact with the net.

Note: Any type of equipment or jewelry which, in the judgement of the referee, is deemed to be unsafe and presenting a potential for injury to the wearer, or any other participant in the match, may not be worn.

Shoes. Shoes may be worn in competition on grass courts. It is illegal to wear shoes with any type of cleats. For competition on sand courts, it is illegal to wear shoes. Socks or booties may be worn to protect the feet if the sand is hot.

Substitutions. No substitutions are permitted for doubles teams.

For teams consisting of three or more players, substitutions may be as follows: a) Before the start of each match, including during tournament play, teams shall submit a roster listing all team members and the uniform number each player and substitute will wear.

Rosters shall also indicate the head coach, who must sign the roster. Once the roster has been submitted to the second referee or scorekeeper no changes may be made;

b) At least two minutes before the start of a match and prior to the expiration of the intermission between games, the head coach or team captain shall submit to the scorekeeper or second referee a signed lineup of players in the service order each will play.

Lineups will be submitted on the official lineup sheet. After the lineup sheets have been received by the scorekeeper, no changes may be made.

Errors in recording lineups on the scoresheet may be corrected if necessitated due to a scorekeeper's error. Players listed on the lineup sheets may be replaced prior to the start of play through a substitution request by the head coach or captain under the provisions of "e" below. One of the players on the lineup sheet must be designated as the playing captain. Prior to the start of play, opponents will not be permitted to see the lineup submitted by the opposing team;

c) Substitutions may be requested by either the playing captain on the court or the head coach when the ball is dead. A team is allowed a maximum of six team substitutions in any one game.

Before entering the game, a substitute must report to the second referee in proper playing uniform ready to immediately enter when authorization is given. If the substitution is not completed immediately, the substitution shall be canceled and the team charged with a delay (team yellow card).

No additional request may be made until after the next dead ball, or a team has been granted a time-out;

d) The playing captain or head coach requesting a substitution(s) shall indicate the number of substitutions desired and shall report to the second referee the jersey numbers of players involved in the substitution.

If the head coach or playing captain fails to indicate that more than one substitution is desired, the first or second referee shall permit only one substitute to enter and charge the team with an improper request. Following a completed substitution, a team may not make a new request for substitution until the next dead ball or until a time-out has been requested and granted to either team.

During a legal charged team time-out, any number of requests for substitution may be made by either team. Immediately following a time-out period, an additional request for substitution may be made;

e) Players starting a game may be replaced only once by a substitute and may subsequently enter the game once, but in the original position in the serving order in relation to other players. Only a starting player may replace a substitute during the same game.

There may be a maximum of two players participating in any one position in the service order (except in case of accident or injury requiring abnormal substitution under the provisions of "g" below).

If an improper substitution request is made (i.e. excess team or player substitution, second request for substitution during the same dead ball period, etc.) the request will be refused and the team charged with an improper request. No new request may be made until the next dead ball or one of the teams has been granted a time-out.

Injuries. Players injured during doubles competition may be granted a three-minute injury time-out.

If a player becomes injured in other than doubles competition and cannot continue playing within 15 seconds, the player must be replaced by a substitute or the team must take a time-out if the player is to remain in the game. If the player is replaced, regardless of time required to safely remove the player from the court, no time-out shall be charged.

If through accident or injury a player is unable to play and substitution cannot be made (as noted above), or if the team has used its allowable six team substitutions, such player may be replaced in the following priority without penalty:

1) By any substitute who has not participated in the game.

2) By the substitute who played in the position of the injured player.

3) By any substitute, regardless of position previously played. Players removed from the game under abnormal substitution provisions, or substitutes whose injuries create an abnormal sub-

stitution due to their inability to enter the game to replace an injured player, will not be permitted to participate in the remainder of the game.

If through injury or accident a player is unable to play and substitution cannot be made according to the provisions above, the referee may grant a special time-out of up to three minutes. Play will be resumed as soon as the injured player is able to continue. In no case shall the special injury time-out exceed three minutes.

At the end of the special time-out, a team may request a normal time-out provided they have not already used their allowable two time-outs. If, after three minutes, or at the expiration of time-outs granted subsequent to the special time-out, the injured player cannot continue to play, the team loses the game by default, keeping any points acquired.

No player may be granted more than one three-minute injury time-out during any match.

If a player becomes injured to the extent that a second injury time-out would be required, the match shall be defaulted for the safety of the player.

If a team becomes incomplete through expulsion or disqualification of a player, and substitution cannot be made under the provisions outlined above, the team loses the game by default, keeping any points acquired.

Note: Injury time-outs are not considered one of the time-outs permitted each team under the U.S. rules. Under AVP rules, an injured player is permitted a five-minute recovery time.

If the player is not ready to play within five minutes, the team must use its available time-outs. If the team has no remaining time-outs, the opponents are awarded one point for each one-minute increment necessary for recovery of the injured player.

TEAM AREAS, DURATION OF MATCH, AND INTERRUPTIONS OF PLAY

Coin Toss. Prior to the start of a game, a coin toss will be used to determine which team has the choice of options. The winner of the toss may elect to serve, receive, or take choice of court for the first game:

a) if the winner chooses to serve or receive, the other team has choice of court for the first game; b) if the winner takes choice of court, the other team has the choice or serving or receiving first for the first game; or c) for subsequent games of the match, the loser of the initial coin toss receives first choice of options.

Number of Games. Matches may consist of a single game or the best of two out of three games. No other format is permitted.

Prematch Warmups. Teams shall have shared use of the court for 15 minutes unless such time is shortened by the Tournament Director due to time restrictions for completion of play.

Time Between Games. The interval between games of a match shall not exceed five minutes.

Interruptions. A player may stop play by calling "ball on" if a ball, other than the game ball, is on or has been on the court during play. A replay will be directed unless, in the judgment of referee, the ball did not interfere with a reasonable playing of the ball.

Winning Score and Changing Sides. A game may consist of eleven or fifteen points. A team wins the game when it reaches the score and has at least a two-point advantage. There is no point cap and rally point scoring is not used in a deciding game of a match.

Teams change areas when reaching multiples of five points when playing fifteen point games.

Teams change areas when reaching multiples of four points when playing eleven point games.

Note: Teams are permitted 30 seconds in which to change courts.

COMMENCEMENT OF PLAY AND THE SERVICE

When the Ball Becomes Alive. The ball become alive and in play at the moment of contact during a legal service.

Dead Ball. The ball remains dead if contacted illegally for service. A live ball becomes dead when: a) a player commits a fault, or; b) when the referee stops play. If a fault occurs after the ball has hit the ground, but during the player's normal "continuation of play," the fault shall be called. The referee will determine when play has ended.

The Service. The service is the act of putting the ball into play. The ball must be hit cleanly with one hand or arm. The server may not step on, touch, or step under the court end line before contacting the ball for service.

Service may be made from any point behind the end line.

Serving Out of Order. For other than doubles competition, if a team has served out of order, the team loses the service and any points gained while serving out of order if it is discovered before the opponents serve. The players of the team at fault must immediately resume their correct positions on the court.

For doubles competition, if a player is discovered serving out of order, the same server continues to serve with no loss of points. Upon receiving the ball for the next term of service, the teammate will serve and the alternating of servers resumes.

The object is to prevent one player from serving three consecutive terms of service.

121

Positions at Service. In doubles and triples competition, players may be positioned anywhere within their court. There is no requirement for players to be in any specific position in relationship to the service order.

For other types of competition, at the time the ball is contacted for the serve, the placement of players must conform to the service order recorded on the scoresheet as follows (the server is exempt from this requirement):

In the front or back row, the center player may not be as near the right sideline as the right player or as near the left sideline as the left player. No back row player may be as near the net as the corresponding front row player. After the ball is contacted for the serve, players may move from their respective positions.

The serving order, as recorded on the official scoresheet, must remain the same until the game is completed.

Before the start of a new game, the serving order may be changed and such changes must be recorded on the scoresheet. It is the responsibility of the head coach or team captain to submit a signed lineup to the scorekeeper prior to the expiration of the authorized rest period between games of a match.

PLAYING THE BALL

Ball Inbounds. A ball that lands on or inside a boundary line or causes the line to bounce is considered to have landed inbounds. On sand courts, the referee may check for ball marks before ruling a ball "inbounds" or "out of bounds." During such check, players must remain on their own court and well away from the area being checked.

Ball Out of Bounds. A ball that touches a net support post or other object outside the court is considered to be out of bounds.

Ball Crossing the Net. The ball must cross the net or net support cables clearly inside the vertical extension of the net support posts. A ball, other than a served ball, contacting the net or support cables remains in play.

Team Contacts. A team is permitted three contacts to return the ball to the opponents. Blocking does not constitute a team contact.

Player Contact. A player may contact the ball with any part of the body, to include that part below the waist.

The ball must rebound cleanly and may not come to rest or roll along a player's body. When defending a hard spiked ball, the ball can be held overhand with the fingers briefly as a reflex action, but not as a planned action.

A player may contact the ball only once during any single effort to play the ball.

Exceptions: A player may have successive (multiple) contacts of the ball during blocking or during a single attempt to make the first team hit of a ball coming from the opponents. AVP and WPVA rules count blocking as a team hit. Teams are limited to two additional contacts of the ball.

Setting. The ball may be contacted with open hands above the shoulder during an overhand pass, provided such contact is simultaneous. The ball may be directed in any direction after such contact.

Rotation of the ball is not considered to be a fault.

If the ball is intentionally set into the opponents' court, the ball must be contacted above the shoulders and must be directed behind or in front of the direction the upper torso is facing.

Comment: Efforts are being made to eliminate lifts occurring during "beach digs" or "deep dish sets." Intentionally sidesetting the ball across the net is illegal. It is not a fault if the ball is set to a teammate and the ball is caused to float over the net.

Dinking. When dinking or tapping the ball, the ball must be cleanly hit with the heel or palm of the hand ("roll shot"), with straight locked fingertips ("the cobra"), or closed or knurled fingers ("camel toe"). Open-hand placement or redirecting the ball is prohibited.

Blocking Faults. In doubles competition, there are no front and back row players. Therefore, there are no back-row blocker faults possible.

PLAY AT THE NET

Playing Ball Under the Net. A ball crossing the center line below the net may be returned by the attacking team, provided the ball has not passed beyond the plane of the net or contacted an opposing player.

Crossing Center Line. Players may cross the centerline below the net provided there is no interference with opponents. A player may enter the opponent's court fully beyond the center line.

Incidental contact with an opponent is ignored unless such contact interferes with the opponent's opportunity to play the ball.

It is legal for a player to contact the ball beyond the center line outside the court provided the ball is returned outside the net to the player's area.

Simultaneous Contact Between Opponents. If players of opposing teams cause the ball to come to rest above the net, it is not a fault and play shall continue.

REFEREES

First Referee. The first referee may stand on the ground or on a stand which elevates the head approximately one-half meter (18" to 24") above the height of the net.

Second Referee. The second referee, if one is assigned, shall be positioned outside the net support post.

PRODUCT SOURCES

The following is a short sampling of companies offering backyard game equipment through the mail:

World Wide Games
Mill Street
Colchester, CT 06415
Catlalog free.
Toll-free telephone: 1-800-243-9232
An excellent selection of quality games including marbles, volleyball, petanque, and many others.

Langenbach
P.O. Box 453
Blairstown, NJ 07825
Toll-free telephone: 1-800-362-1991
Although primarily a catalog of quality garden tools, Langenbach also carries top-of-the-line croquet, bocce, and horseshoe sets, as well as an adjustable tetherball system.

Plow & Hearth
301 Madison Road
P.O. Box 830
Orange, VA 229060-0492
Toll-free telephone: 1-800-627-1712
All sorts of things for backyard life including croquet, horseshoe, and bocce sets, a portable volleyball set, and a large, heavy-duty plastic storage box (called a "Deck Box") for storing games and other equipment.

John Deere Catalog
1400 Third Avenue
Moline, IL 61265
Toll-free telephone: 1-800-544-2122
A wide array of items for backyard fun including horseshoes and ready-made stilts.

ASSOCIATIONS

United States Badminton Association
1750 East Boulder Street,
    Building 10, Room 127
Colorado Springs, Colorado 80909
Telephone: (719) 578-4808

International Bocce Association
187 Proctor Boulevard
Utica, New York 13501
Telephone: (315) 733-9611

United States Croquet Association
500 Avenue of the Champions
Palm Beach Gardens, Florida 33418
Telephone: (407) 627-3999

National Horseshoe Pitchers Association
c/o Mr. Donnie Roberts
Box 7927
Columbus, Ohio 43207
Telephone: (614) 444-8510

American Lawn Bowls Association
c/o Merton Isaacman
17 Buckthorn
Irvine, California 92714
Telephone: (714) 476-3133

National Shuffleboard Association
c/o Howard Rayle
704 52nd Avenue Drive West
Bradenton, Florida 34207
Telephone: (813) 753-9061

United States Volleyball Association
3595 East Fountain Boulevard, Suite I-2
Colorado Springs, Colorado 80910-1740
Telephone: (719) 637-8300

INDEX

INDEX

INDEX

About This Book

The body text of this book is set in Adobe Garamond Regular. The sidebars and captions are set in Adobe Garamond Italic. The illustration notes are set in a modified hand-lettered typeface called Tekton. *Backyard Games* was designed and composed on a Macintosh computer system.

About the Author

A. Cort Sinnes was a part of the original creative team for Ortho Books, for whom he wrote ten books on gardening and outdoor living. He is the former editor of *Flower & Garden* magazine and the author of *In Your Own Backyard* and *The Grilling Encyclopedia.* Sinnes's syndicated newspaper column, concerning the joys of backyard living, appears in some 250 newspapers nationwide. He resides in his hometown in California's Napa Valley with his wife and 13-year-old daughter.